FROM PRISON TO HOME:

The Dimensions and

Consequences of

Prisoner Reentry

Jeremy Travis

Amy L. Solomon

Michelle Waul

June 2001

About the Authors

Jeremy Travis is a senior fellow at the Urban Institute, developing research and policy agendas on crime in the community context, new concepts of the agencies of justice, sentencing and prisoner reentry, and international crime. Mr. Travis is co-chair of the Reentry Roundtable, a group of prominent academics, practitioners, service providers, and community leaders working to advance policies and innovations on prisoner reentry that reflect solid research. Before he joined the Urban Institute, Mr. Travis was the director of the National Institute of Justice, the research arm of the U.S. Department of Justice. Mr. Travis has been an active figure in the development of a policy and research agenda on the issue of prisoner reentry. He is the author of the article "But They All Come Back: Rethinking Prisoner Reentry," and shaped the federal initiative on reentry courts and reentry partnerships. Mr. Travis earned his JD, cum laude, from the New York University School of Law; an MPA from the New York University Wagner Graduate School of Public Service; and a BA in American Studies, cum laude, with honors from Yale College.

Amy L. Solomon is a policy associate at the Urban Institute, where she works to link the research activities of the Justice Policy Center to policy and practice arenas in the field. Her primary areas of concentration are prisoner reentry and problem-solving approaches to public safety. She currently serves as project manager for the Reentry Roundtable and co-manages a project for the U.S. Department of Health and Human Services that focuses on the impact of incarceration and reentry on children, families, and low-income communities. Before she joined the Urban Institute, Ms. Solomon served as policy analyst and acting director of strategic planning at the National Institute of Justice, the research arm of the U.S. Department of Justice. There, she developed and managed prisoner reentry and community crime reduction initiatives; prepared background papers for senior department officials; and provided a research basis for emerging crime policy initiatives. Prior to her work at the Justice Department, Ms. Solomon managed a community service program for offenders; developed strategies for prisoners transitioning to the community; worked with juveniles in detention, probation, and school settings; and participated in various criminal justice working groups, boards, and committees. Ms. Solomon has an MPP degree with a concentration in criminal justice policy and management from Harvard University's Kennedy School of Government.

Michelle Waul is a research associate with the Justice Policy Center. She focuses on initiatives to help inform the work of policymakers and practitioners by facilitating links to the research activities of the Center. Her primary areas of concentration are violent crime victimization and offending, prisoner reentry, transnational crime, and understanding crime in the community context. She co-manages a reentry project, funded by the U.S. Department of Health and Human Services, assessing the impact of incarceration and return of ex-prisoners on children, families, and low-income communities. Her other Urban Institute projects have included drafting data collection instruments and a literature review for a national evaluation of the Victims of Crime Act program. Before she joined the Urban Institute, Ms. Waul served as the project manager for the Victims of Crime Act program for the state of Illinois. Ms. Waul has an MPP degree from Georgetown University's Public Policy Institute and a BA in sociology and criminal justice from the University of Wisconsin at Madison.

FROM PRISON TO HOME:

The Dimensions and
Consequences of
Prisoner Reentry

Contents

Acknowledgments

The authors would like to thank the many individuals who made valuable contributions to this monograph. We thank Joan Petersilia, Bill Sabol, Todd Clear, Ed Rhine, and Mike Thompson for reviewing and commenting on an early draft. Their insightful feedback and varied perspectives on prisoner reentry helped make this a more comprehensive document. Several colleagues here at the Urban Institute made important contributions as well: Alexa Hirst, Jake Rosenfeld, and Sarah Lawrence provided data, text, sources, and valuable edits, big and small. Adele Harrell, director of the Justice Policy Center, was a critical reader and provided staff resources that made this monograph possible. Christy Visher, Peter Reuter, Laura Winterfield, and Shelli Rossman read versions of the report and provided constructive guidance along the way. David Williams, our graphics guru, transformed the document from words on a page into a professional and accessible document that others might just want to read. Finally, we would like to thank the Open Society Institute's Center on Crime, Communities, and Culture, and Susan Tucker in particular, for supporting the first meeting of the Reentry Roundtable in October 2000 and the production of this report. The Roundtable discussions, its members, and the commissioned papers provided the foundation and the impetus for the development of this monograph. In the spirit of the Reentry Roundtable, we encourage the readers of this report to contact us with new research findings or promising policy innovations so that the national discussion of prisoner reentry is further enriched.

Prisoner Reentry: An Overview

INTRODUCTION

About 600,000 individuals—roughly 1,600 a day—will be released from state and federal prisons this year to return to their communities.[1] On one level, this transition from prison to community might be viewed as unremarkable. Ever since prisons were built, individuals have faced the challenges of moving from confinement in correctional institutions to liberty on the street.

Yet, from a number of policy perspectives, the age-old issue of prisoner reintegration is taking on new importance. More prisoners are returning home, having spent longer terms behind bars, less prepared for life on the outside, with less assistance in their reintegration. Often they will have difficulties reconnecting with jobs, housing, and perhaps their families when they return, and will remain beset by substance abuse and health problems. Most will be rearrested, and many will be returned to prison for new crimes or parole violations. And this cycle of removal and return of large numbers of individuals, mostly men, is increasingly concentrated in a relatively small number of communities that already encounter enormous social and economic disadvantages.

The costs of this cycle of incarceration and reentry are high from several perspectives. First and foremost is the public safety dimension. Nearly two-thirds of released prisoners are expected to be rearrested for a felony or serious misdemeanor within three years of their release. Such high recidivism rates translate into thousands of new victimizations each year. Second, there are fiscal implications. Significant portions of state budgets are now invested in the criminal justice system. Expenditures on corrections alone increased from $9 billion in 1982 to $44 billion in 1997.[2] These figures do not include the cost of arrest and sentencing processes, nor do they take into account the cost to victims. Third, there are far-reaching social costs. Prisoner reentry carries the potential for profound collateral consequences, including public health risks, disenfranchisement, homelessness, and weakened ties among families and communities.

But just as the costs are great, so too are the opportunities. Managing reentry so that fewer crimes are committed would enhance public safety. Managing reentry so that there are fewer returns to prison would translate into

Reentry Defined

We define "reentry" as the process of leaving prison and returning to society. All prisoners experience reentry irrespective of their method of release or form of supervision, if any. So both prisoners who are released on parole and those who are released when their prison term expires experience reentry.

If the reentry process is successful, there are benefits in terms of both public safety and the long-term reintegration of the ex-prisoner. Public safety gains are typically measured in terms of reduced recidivism. Reintegration outcomes would include increased participation in social institutions such as the labor force, families, communities, schools, and religious institutions. There are financial and social benefits associated with both kinds of improvements.

Throughout this monograph, we principally address reentry as it relates to adult state prisons. While the concept of reentry is applicable in various contexts involving a transition from any type of incarceration to freedom—from jails, federal prisons, juvenile facilities, or even pretrial detention—we focus here on the reentry of state prisoners back to the community. We have limited our scope to state prisons in order to focus on individuals who have been convicted of the most serious offenses, who have been removed from communities for longer periods of time, and who are managed by state correctional and parole systems.

significant cost savings. Managing reentry to achieve long-term reintegration would have far-reaching benefits for the families and communities most affected by reentry, as well as for former prisoners. These interrelated opportunities bring the stakes of reentry into view. There is much to be gained.

The costs and opportunities also raise important questions about what we can do to prepare both ex-prisoners and their communities for their inevitable return home. How can public resources best be allocated to improve public safety and prevent reoffending? How can we craft strategies that increase the odds of successful prisoner reintegration? What types of policies can realistically be implemented to make a difference in the short term?

In an effort to seek answers to these important questions, the Urban Institute hosted the first "Reentry Roundtable" meeting in October 2000. With funding support from the Open Society Institute, we brought together a diverse group of academics and practitioners to assess the state of knowledge about these issues. The Urban Institute commissioned research papers on various dimensions of reentry—from substance abuse, health, and labor market issues to the impact of reentry on families, children, and communities. And we engaged in a two-day discussion about the research and policy opportunities before us. (See sidebar on the Reentry Roundtable for a list of participants and discussion papers.)

Based on that meeting, the discussion papers commissioned for the meeting, and additional literature from the field, we have created this report. We aim to highlight relevant research and identify key issues that most warrant policy attention. In this report, we describe the reentry process, the challenges for reentry, and the consequences of reentry along several key dimensions. Throughout, we convey research findings and identify strategic policy and research opportunities. We hope that the information presented here will help lay the groundwork for further research and, most important, for future policy innovation.

Reentry Roundtable

October 2000 meeting participants:

Jeremy Travis (Co-chair), Urban Institute

Joan Petersilia (Co-chair), University of California at Irvine

James Austin, George Washington University

Todd Clear, John Jay College of Criminal Justice

Tony Fabelo, Texas Criminal Justice Policy Council

Joe Frye, Safer Foundation

Gerald Gaes, Federal Bureau of Prisons

John Hagan, Northwestern University

Theodore Hammett, Abt Associates

Adele Harrell, Urban Institute

Lana Harrison, University of Delaware

Sally Hillsman, National Institute of Justice

Martin Horn, Pennsylvania Department of Corrections

Sharon Jackson, California Department of Corrections

Jeffrey Kling, Princeton University

John Laub, University of Maryland

Joseph Lehman, Washington Department of Corrections

James Lynch, American University

Larry Meachum, Department of Justice Corrections Program Office

Sam Myers, University of Minnesota

Paul Offner, Georgetown University

Fred Osher, University of Maryland

Ed Rhine, Ohio Department of Rehabilitation and Correction

Beth Richie, University of Illinois at Chicago

William Sabol, Case Western Reserve University

Michael Sarbanes, Office of the Lieutenant Governor, State of Maryland

Rick Seiter, St. Louis University

Carol Shapiro, Family Justice

Susan Tucker, Open Society Institute

Bruce Western, Princeton University

Reginald Wilkinson, Ohio Department of Rehabilitation and Correction

Diane Williams, Safer Foundation

Discussion papers commissioned for the Reentry Roundtable:

- "Prisoner Reentry: Current Trends, Practices, and Issues," by James Austin, George Washington University

- "Returning Captives of the American War on Drugs: Issues of Community and Family Reentry," by John Hagan, Northwestern University, and Juleigh Petty, American Bar Foundation

- "Coercive Mobility and the Community: The Impact of Removing and Returning Offenders," by Todd Clear, Dina Rose, and Judith A. Ryder, John Jay College of Criminal Justice

- "The Challenge of Reintegrating Drug Offenders in the Community," by Lana Harrison, University of Delaware

- "Health-Related Issues in Prisoner Reentry to the Community," by Theodore Hammett, Abt Associates

- "Issues Incarcerated Women Face When They Return to Their Communities," by Beth Ritchie, University of Illinois at Chicago

- "The Labor Market Consequences of 'Mass' Incarceration," by Jeffrey Kling and Bruce Western, Princeton University, and David Weiman, Russell Sage Foundation

Extant papers used for the Reentry Roundtable and circulated with the commissioned papers:

- "Prisoners Returning to Communities: Political, Economic, and Social Consequences," by Joan Petersilia, University of California-Irvine

- "But They All Come Back: Rethinking Prisoner Reentry," by Jeremy Travis, Urban Institute

- "State and Federal Prisoners Returning to the Community: Findings from the Bureau of Justice Statistics," by Allen Beck, U.S. Department of Justice

These discussion papers will be published, in expanded versions, in a special edition of *Crime and Delinquency*. The volume will also include a new paper on the role of victims in prisoner reentry, by Susan Herman and Cressida Wasserman of the National Center for Victims of Crime; a paper on the mental health consequences of incarceration and reentry, by Arthur Lurigio of Loyola University; and an introductory essay on the policy implications of the reentry perspective, by Jeremy Travis and Joan Petersilia. The special issue is scheduled for publication in July 2001. To order a copy, go to http://www.sagepub.com/shopping/journal.asp?id=4704.

SENTENCING AND SUPERVISION CONTEXT

Over the past generation, sentencing policy in the United States has been characterized by three major developments. The first is a remarkable increase in U.S. imprisonment rates. There are now more than a million people in state and federal prisons—a fourfold increase since 1973.[3] The second is a shift in sentencing and supervision policy away from indeterminate sentencing and earned release to greater (but not universal) reliance on determinate sentencing and mandatory release. Third, the system of parole supervision has undergone significant changes, with increasing caseloads, new monitoring capacities, and an increased focus on surveillance over rehabilitation. Taken together, these trends place an increased burden on the formal and informal processes that should work together to support successful reintegration.

The per capita rate of imprisonment in America hovered at about 110 per 100,000 from 1925 to 1973, with little variation.[4] Starting in 1973, however, the rate of imprisonment has grown steadily, so that in 1999 there were 476 incarcerated individuals for every 100,000 residents—more than four times the 1973 level.[5] As a result, state prisons now house 1,200,000 individuals and federal prisons house 135,000. Another 605,000 persons are held in local jails.[6]

The impact of this growth in incarceration rates on prisoner reentry is clear—the more people we put in prison, the more will eventually come out.[7] Over the past two decades, the number of prisoners released each year has grown nearly fourfold, from 147,895 in 1977 to an estimated 585,000 in 2000.[8]

In 1999, 476 persons per 100,000 residents were sentenced to at least a year's confinement—equivalent to 1 in every 110 men and 1 in every 1,695 women. These rates vary dramatically by race. In 1999, 1 in every 29 African-American males was sentenced to at least a year's confinement, compared with 1 in every 75 Hispanic males, and 1 in every 240 white males. One in every 472 African-American females was sentenced to at least a year's confinement, compared with 1 in every 1,149 Hispanic females, and 1 in every 3,704 white females.[9]

Figure 1. Sentenced Prisoners Admitted and Released from State and Federal Prisons, 1977–98

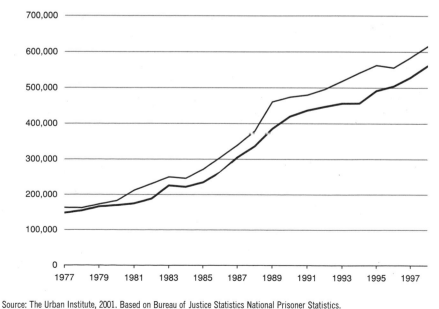

Source: The Urban Institute, 2001. Based on Bureau of Justice Statistics National Prisoner Statistics.

Over the same period, the overarching jurisprudential and penal philosophy that once guided the reentry process, namely the philosophy of rehabilitation and earned reintegration within a framework of indeterminate sentencing, lost its intellectual and policy dominance.[10] Under the indeterminate approach, state statutes provided broad ranges of possible sentences, authorized the release of prisoners by parole boards, and explicitly embraced rehabilitation of prisoners as the goal of corrections. Starting in the mid-1970s, critics from different ideological and intellectual perspectives began arguing for changes in this approach, for different reasons. For instance, civil rights activists and defense lawyers, citing evidence of widespread racial and class disparities in sentencing and correctional administration, called for limiting the discretion of judges and other correctional authorities in sentencing matters. On the other hand, political conservatives pointed to rising crime rates and research findings that questioned the effectiveness of rehabilitation and advocated sentencing reforms as a means to enforce tougher standards and crack down on criminals.[11] This ideological and political shift away from the framework of indeterminate sentencing has had significant effects on federal and state sentencing policy. The unifying sentencing approach of the past has been replaced with a variety of state-level experiments in mandatory minimums, abolition of discretionary parole release, three-strikes laws, sex offender registration, sharply reduced judicial discretion, and truth-in-sentencing policies, among others.[12]

Such staples of correctional management as good-time credits earned through compliance with requirements and successful completion of in-prison programming and discretionary release through review by a parole board have been abolished or curtailed in many states. Further, intensive case planning and management, both pre- and post-release, and the availability of community support services have not been viewed as priorities. For example, recent surveys of parole officers show that more of them give high priority to the law enforcement function of parole, rather than its service or rehabilitation function.[13] At the same time, the level of per capita spending for parole supervision has been reduced[14] and parole caseloads per officer have risen.[15] New surveillance capabilities—including electronic monitoring and drug testing—have been introduced, providing enhanced capacity to detect parole violations and to increase the rate of revocations.[16]

For these and other reasons, the rate of parole violations has increased significantly over recent years. In 1985, 70 percent of parolees successfully completed their parole term; by 1998, the number had dropped to 45 percent. As a result, parole revocations now account for more than a third of prison admissions, up from 18 percent in 1980.[17] Indeed, parole violators are the fastest growing category of prison admissions.[18]

In summary, the burden on the systems that manage reentry has increased substantially and the operational capacity to manage these increases has not kept pace. Furthermore, as discussed later in this report, the increase in the number of prison releases has placed significantly greater strains on the same communities where prisoner removal and return are most concentrated.

Most of the figures reported throughout the monograph are national totals or averages, and therefore they mask the varying trends that exist at the state level. For example, 531,312 persons were released from state prisons in the United States in 1998. Not surprisingly, these releases were not distributed evenly across states. California alone accounted for some 130,000 state prison releases, or 24 percent of all releases nationally, while Montana accounted for 1,100 releases, just one-fifth of 1 percent. Figure 2 illustrates the variation in the number of prisoners released per state. Throughout the report, we will provide examples and maps that illustrate this variation.

Figure 2. Number of Releases from Prison, by State, 1998

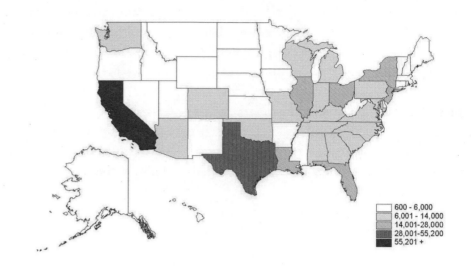

	600 - 6,000
	6,001 - 14,000
	14,001-28,000
	28,001-55,200
	55,201 +

Source: The Urban Institute, 2001. Based on Bureau of Justice Statistics National Prisoner Statistics.

REENTRY AND PUBLIC SAFETY

Individual rates of reoffending after incarceration are high. Based on available research, nearly two-thirds of all released prisoners are expected to be rearrested within three years. The impact of recidivism by returning prisoners is disproportionately felt among a relatively small number of disadvantaged communities. Some might suggest that an appropriate response would be to impose longer prison terms to keep offenders out of the community for longer periods. While there are crime control effects from incarceration, recent research shows that more prison expansion would produce only minimal gains in public safety. Viewed from a different perspective, one study found that beyond a certain "tipping point" in some communities, increasing levels of incarceration may actually lead to increases in crime through a weakening of informal, social controls. The challenge is to understand how to effectively manage the inevitable returns from prison so that communities will be safer. This may require a careful look at differential risks posed by former prisoners, new strategies for parole, and crime control tactics that reduce reliance on incarceration.

The release of prisoners back into their communities poses two fundamentally interrelated challenges: First, how to protect the safety of the public, and second, how to foster an individual's transition from life in prison to life as a productive citizen. Even though these dimensions of reentry are related, it is useful to differentiate the potential benefits to public safety from the broader benefits to communities and former prisoners that successful reintegration promises. In this section, we focus on the former—the contribution of released prisoners to crime. As discussed above, some 600,000 prisoners are released from prison each year and the majority who are under supervision fail while on parole. But to what extent is this population actually committing new crimes and endangering the community? Relatedly, how much additional safety can be produced by more effective reentry strategies?

Given the centrality of this question to the development of policies to guide prisoner reentry, it is remarkable how little research has been conducted on the topic. In 1989, the Bureau of Justice Statistics (BJS) published the largest study on recidivism of released prisoners.[19] The researchers tracked a large sample of prisoners released from 11 states in 1983 and measured their recidivism rates over the following three-year period. The 11 states accounted for more than half of all state prison releases (57 percent) in the United States that year. During those three years, 63 percent of the 1983 release cohort were rearrested at least once for a felony or serious misdemeanor; 47 percent were reconvicted; and 41 percent of the release cohort were reincarcerated. Individuals were most likely to reoffend during their first year out of prison—40 percent were rearrested within that first year.

According to the study, an estimated 68,000 of the released prisoners were arrested and charged with some 327,000 felonies and serious misdemeanors, including 50,000 violent offenses; 141,000 property offenses; 46,000 drug offenses; and 80,000 public order offenses over the ensuing three years.[20] More than 93,000 of these arrests are classified as Uniform Crime Reports Index crimes (i.e., murder and nonnegligent manslaughter, rape, robbery, aggravated assault, burglary, larceny, and motor vehicle theft). The group of prisoners released in 1983 accounted for 3.9 percent of all arrests for Index crimes in the 11 states over the first six months, and 2.8 percent of all arrests for Index crimes over that three-year time period.[21] It is important to note that this 2.8 percent contribution accounts only for the arrests of prisoners released in 1983. For example, it does not factor in the extent to which prisoners released in 1981 or 1982 contributed to arrests in 1983. In addition, these recidivism rates capture only those offenses that were reported to the police (typically just over one-third of victimizations are reported to the police[22]) *and* resulted in an arrest. Therefore, reoffending rates among ex-inmates are higher than those reported in this study; additionally, the contribution of their rates to the overall crime rate are more substantial and their impacts on certain communities are even more pronounced. Finally, it is not known whether the increase in the country's annual releases since 1983 has resulted in proportional increases in crimes that are attributable to this group.

The public safety risks posed by the returning population can also be viewed through a community lens. As discussed in Chapter 4 of this report, individuals leaving prison return to a relatively small number of neighborhoods concentrated within the nation's large cities. This concentration of individuals at a high risk of reoffending may present opportunities, as well as the obvious risks. For example, the development of "place-based" crime reduction strategies, now

Research on Recidivism Among Released Offenders

While more research is needed to estimate the contributions of recently released prisoners to the crime rates in different communities, two studies by the Bureau of Justice Statistics (BJS) shed light on the issue.

The first study tracks samples of felony arrestees in the 75 largest counties. The most recently published data are for 1996 felony arrestees.[23] BJS found that 6 percent of felony arrestees were on parole at the time of arrest. The second study is the *Survey of State and Federal Inmates,* conducted every few years by BJS, which indicates that 24 percent of the prison population in 1997 were on parole at the time they committed the offense that led to incarceration.

The first survey reflects only arrests, so it does not account for crime rates generally. The second sample reflects the prison population, not a representative sample of offenders.

BJS is currently conducting a new recidivism study that tracks prisoners released in 1994 in 15 states. Analysis from this study will be published in 2001 and will help shape our understanding about individual recidivism and contributions to crime.

A review of the research literature reveals how little is known about the ways certain behaviors among certain individuals respond to certain interventions under certain conditions. Acknowledging and addressing individual risk factors are important components in any effective reentry strategy. There may also be situational factors that have an equally important role in predicting successful post-prison adjustment—community factors, state policies, supervision strategies, family structures, availability of jobs, housing, treatment, and the like. To understand the impact of each of these domains on recidivism and reintegration, the Urban Institute is developing a major research project entitled "Returning Home: Understanding the Challenges of Prisoner Reentry." This study will be carried out in up to 11 identified states from 2002 to 2005.

more common among police departments and community crime prevention coalitions, would benefit from a geographic analysis of the safety risks posed and barriers faced by returning prisoners. Even marginal gains in individual recidivism could translate into noticeable safety gains in the communities experiencing high rates of prisoner reentry. In Boston, for example, the crime reduction strategies known as "Operation Ceasefire" focused attention on the behaviors of individuals under criminal justice supervision in a small number of neighborhoods and resulted in substantial improvements.[24] Boston is currently adapting the Ceasefire model to address the issue of prisoner reentry.

The reentry phenomenon and the attendant safety risks should also be viewed through the lens of the prisoner's family. Arguably, as the number of prison releases increases, the impact of recidivism may be disproportionately felt by families with histories of violence within the home. Some former prisoners, whether convicted of domestic violence or other crimes, may pose a risk to the families to which they return. Yet remarkably little is known about the effects returning prisoners have on incidences of domestic violence and child abuse, so these issues clearly warrant further attention.

How should society respond to the high rates of reoffending among released prisoners? One response could be to continue expanding the use of incarceration. Those favoring this view would cite studies that conclude national prison growth did play a role in recent crime declines. Using different approaches, two researchers estimated that prison expansion may account for approximately 25 percent of the decline, and that up to 75 percent of the crime drop may be attributed to factors other than prison expansion.[25] One of those researchers also suggests that further prison expansion—following the buildup over the last 20 years—would produce only minimal gains in public safety.[26] Of course, any public safety gains would have to be weighed against fiscal and social costs, as well as alternate crime control strategies that could produce the same results.

One provocative new study suggests that more incarceration is counterproductive—that at some point in some neighborhoods, more imprisonment may actually *increase* crime rates. Ironically, these community-level effects are crime-producing, because massive incarceration practices weaken the informal social structures long associated with crime prevention (i.e., strong families, individual and social capital, workforce participation of men in the community) and a tipping point is reached where crime is less inhibited.[27]

Of course, there are ways to manage the public safety risks of returning prisoners other than expanding the prison population. The research literature has identified a number of interventions, such as drug treatment, job training, and educational programs, that have been shown to reduce reoffending rates. Greater investment in these and other proven interventions is needed. In addition, more innovation in the field and evaluation research would help develop strategies that fit the new reality of the large number of prison releases.

Within state budgets, there is a tension between different spending priorities, such as higher education and corrections. Nationally, state spending on corrections increased 1,200 percent between 1973 and 1993 to build prisons and house new prisoners, while spending on higher education increased only 419 percent despite a similar boom in university enrollments.[28]

The Reentry Process

More than 95 percent of the nation's state prisoners will eventually return to the community. In fact, some 40 percent of those currently in state prisons will be released within the next 12 months.[29] What do we know about the processes and circumstances under which inmates are being released? This section describes the characteristics of returning prisoners, how release decisions are made, how prisoners are prepared for release and reintegration, the "moment of release," post-prison supervision, and the growing frequency of parole revocation.

WHO'S COMING HOME?[30]

The population of returning prisoners is generally at high risk along several critical dimensions. Of the nearly 600,000 inmates returning to communities across the country each year, most have not completed high school, have limited employment skills, and have histories of substance abuse and health problems. Today, there are substantially more individuals released from prison having served a term for a drug-related or violent offense.[31] About one-third of all prisoners are released following a conviction for a drug offense (up from 11 percent in 1985). One-fourth are released following a conviction for a violent offense (down from 32 percent in 1985). Returning prisoners have served longer prison sentences than in the past, meaning they may be less attached to jobs, their families, and the communities to which they return.

The large majority of returning prisoners are male (88 percent), although the percentage of women in the parole population has risen from 8 to 12 percent over the past decade.[32] The median age is 34 and the median education level is 11th grade.[33] In 1998, more than half of returning prisoners were white (55 percent) and 44 percent were African American. Twenty-one percent of parolees were Hispanic (and may be of any race).[34]

One characteristic of released prisoners that has changed in recent years is the crime for which they were convicted. Looking at all releases from state

Table 1. A Profile of Parolees

Gender	
Male	88%
Female	12%
Race	
White	55%
Black/African American	44%
Other	1%
Hispanic origin	
Hispanic	21%
Non-Hispanic	79%
Age (median)	34 years
Education level (median)	11th grade

Sources: T.P. Bonczar and L.E. Glaze, "Probation and Parole in the United States, 1998." Bureau of Justice Statistics, NCJ 160092, August 1999.

J. Petersilia, "Parole and Prisoner Reentry in the United States." In M. Tonry and J. Petersilia (Eds.), *Prisons.* Chicago: University of Chicago Press, 1999.

and federal prisons, one can see that the number of released prisoners convicted of violent crimes has nearly doubled from 1985 to 1998—from about 75,000 in 1985 to more than 140,000 in 1998—and presumably will continue to increase.[35] However, given the significant increases in the number of prison releases over that same time period, the *share* of individuals released from prison who have been convicted of violent offenses has declined—from approximately 32 percent in 1985 to 25 percent in 1998.

Over the same period, both the number of released prisoners who had been convicted of drug offenses (sales and possession) and their share of the returning population increased significantly. The number of released drug offenders rose from about 25,000 in 1985 to 182,000 in 1998.[36] The proportion of released prisoners who were drug offenders rose from 11 percent in 1985 to 26 percent in 1990 and to 32 percent in 1998.

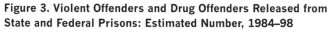

Figure 3. Violent Offenders and Drug Offenders Released from State and Federal Prisons: Estimated Number, 1984–98

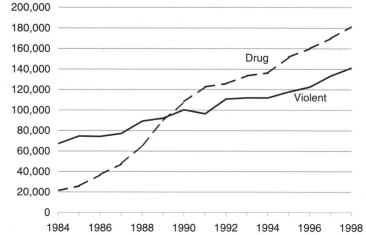

Source: The Urban Institute, 2001. Based on J.P. Lynch and W.J. Sabol, "Prisoner Reentry in Perspective." Urban Institute *Crime Policy Report*, forthcoming; and BJS National Prisoner Statistics.

Figure 4. Violent Offenders and Drug Offenders Released from State and Federal Prisons: Percentage of All Releases, 1984–98

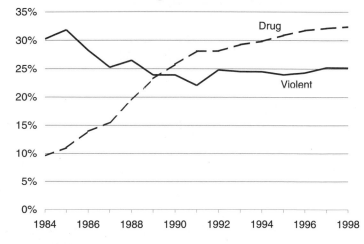

Source: The Urban Institute, 2001. Based on J.P. Lynch and W.J. Sabol, "Prisoner Reentry in Perspective." Urban Institute *Crime Policy Report*, forthcoming; and BJS National Prisoner Statistics.

As a result of sentencing reforms of the past two decades, including man-datory minimums and truth-in-sentencing laws, individuals who are now re-leased from prison have, on average, served longer sentences than prisoners in the past. The amount of time prisoners serve prior to release has increased 27 percent since 1990, from an average of 22 months spent in prison for those released in 1990 to 28 months for those released in 1998.[38]

As figure 5 illustrates, the proportion of soon-to-be-released prisoners who reported they had served five years or more almost doubled between 1991 and 1997—rising from 12 percent to 21 percent over six years. These longer terms translate into further detachment from the communities to which they will return. The share of exiting prisoners who had served between one and five years increased as well, and the percentage of prisoners who served one year or less decreased—from 33 percent in 1991 to 16 percent in 1997.[39]

Figure 5. Prisoners to be Released in the Next 12 Months: Estimated Distribution of Time Served Until Release, 1991 and 1997

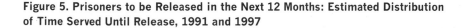

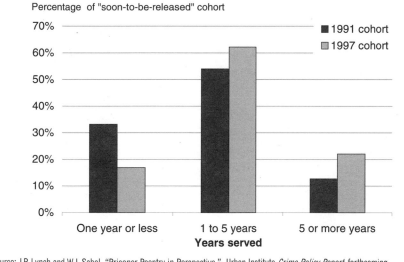

Source: J.P. Lynch and W.J. Sabol, "Prisoner Reentry in Perspective." Urban Institute *Crime Policy Report*, forthcoming.

Returning prisoners are released with a host of health problems. Substance abuse and mental illness are common among soon-to-be-released state prison-ers (i.e., those who are expected to be released within 12 months). About three-quarters of this population have a history of substance abuse, and an estimated 16 percent suffer from mental illness. However, fewer than one-third of exiting prisoners receive substance abuse or mental health treatment while in prison.[40]

A disproportionate share of the prison population also live with chronic health problems or infectious diseases. In 1997, about one-quarter of the indi-viduals living with HIV or AIDS in the United States had been released from a correctional facility (prison or jail) that year. Approximately one-third of those infected with hepatitis C and tuberculosis were released from a prison or jail in 1999. When looked at in terms of the actual prevalence of infectious disease among the prisoners, some 2 to 3 percent of individuals in the prison popula-tion are HIV positive or have AIDS; 18 percent are infected with hepatitis C;

and 7 percent have a TB infection. These infection rates are five to ten times greater than those found in the general U.S. population.[41]

Taken together, the employment, health, substance abuse, education, and housing issues of returning inmates present formidable challenges to successful reintegration. One survey of parolees in California reported that about 85 percent of the state's parole population are chronic drug or alcohol abusers; 70 to 90 percent are unemployed; 50 percent are functionally illiterate; 18 percent have psychiatric problems; and 10 percent are homeless.[42] It is worth noting that most individuals enter prison with these problems. In some cases, prison may actually improve these conditions, not make them worse. For example, prisoners often have greater access to medical care than persons with similar sociodemographic characteristics who are not incarcerated.[43] On the other hand, the prison experience may itself create or exacerbate adverse physical or psychological conditions. Some prisoners experience serious physical injuries and/or psychological trauma while incarcerated. As discussed later in this report, more can be done in prison and upon release to address these various problems and to assist released prisoners in transitioning successfully to life in the community.

Impact of Incarceration and Reentry on African-American Families and Communities

Young, poor, black males are incarcerated at higher rates than any other group, and therefore they are most affected by reentry. The Bureau of Justice Statistics calculated that, in 1991, an African-American male had a 29 percent lifetime chance of serving at least one year in prison, six times higher than that for white males.[44] Hispanic males, who may be of any race, have a lifetime chance of imprisonment of 16 percent.[45] Nine percent of African-American males age 25 to 29 were in prison in 1999, compared with 3 percent of Hispanic males and 1 percent of white males of the same age group.[46] Further, according to one estimate, more than one-third of young, black, male high school dropouts were in prison or jail in the late 1990s—more than were employed.[47]

The disproportionate representation of African Americans in the criminal justice system has been exacerbated by changes in sentencing policy. A 1990 RAND study found that while defendants in California received generally comparable sentences for comparable offenses regardless of race, this was not the case with respect to drug offenses.[48] Sentencing policy changes throughout the 1980s and early 1990s requiring mandatory minimum sentences for a variety of drug-related offenses resulted in a significant increase in drug offenders sentenced to prison and in longer prison terms. This had a significant impact on the African-American state prison population. Overall, the number of black drug offenders sentenced to prison increased by 707 percent between 1985 and 1995, while the number of white drug offenders increased by 306 percent.[49] Drug offenders accounted for 42 percent of the rise in the black state prison population and 26 percent of the rise in the white state prison population during that same 10-year period.[50]

These high rates of incarceration among African Americans have intergenerational consequences. In a 1996 survey of black jail inmates, nearly half indicated that they had a family member who had been incarcerated.[51] Moreover, there is evidence to suggest that children of incarcerated parents are at high risk of future delinquency and/or criminal behavior.[52]

Concentrations in removal and reentry of African-American men also have implications for family formation and stability. In some communities, high rates of incarceration, homicide, and limited employment prospects among African-American males have resulted in an imbalance of marriageable African-American males to females. Some researchers argue that severely imbalanced gender ratios are a predictor of family disruption and a greater likelihood of crime and violence.[53] In addition, Prison Fellowship estimates that only 15 percent of married couples are able to endure a period of incarceration of one partner. Of the 15 percent who do stay together during the prison term, only an estimated 3 to 5 percent are still together one year after release.[54]

Female Prisoners Returning to the Community

Although female prisoners make up only a small portion of the corrections population, they present risks and challenges in many ways more serious and widespread than do their male counterparts.

- *Females represent a small share of the corrections population.* Females accounted for 6 percent of the prison population and 12 percent of the parole population in 1998.[55]

- *Incarceration rates of females are rapidly increasing.* The numbers of females per capita in corrections institutions have grown 48 percent since 1990, compared with a 27 percent per capita increase for men.[56]

A profile of female prisoners

- *The majority of female prisoners are minorities.* Nearly two-thirds (63 percent) of those confined to state prisons are black, Hispanic, or other non-white ethnicity. Minorities make up only 26 percent of the general female population.[57]

- *Female prisoners are more likely to come from lesser economic circumstances than male prisoners.* Thirty-seven percent of females and 28 percent of males had incomes of less than $600 per month prior to arrest. Thirty percent of females and 8 percent of males were receiving welfare assistance prior to arrest.[58]

- *Female prisoners are less likely to be married than the general population.* Nearly half of all women in state prisons have never been married and another 20 percent are divorced.[59] Among the general population, only 21 percent of women 18 or over have never been married.[60]

- *Female prisoners are likely to be parents.* Sixty-five percent of female prisoners have a child below the age of 18. More than 1.3 million children have a mother who is either in prison or under probation or parole supervision.[61]

Challenges facing females returning to the community

- *Many women are released with serious health problems.* Three-and-a-half percent of the female inmate population are HIV positive, a slightly higher percentage than for males. Nearly one-quarter (23 percent) of women in prison receive medication for emotional disorders. More than half of the females (60 percent) in state prisons report a history of physical or sexual abuse.[62]

- *Many women have serious, long-term substance abuse problems.* Increasingly more women are being incarcerated for nonviolent drug offenses (possession and distribution). Forty percent of incarcerated women report that they were under the influence of drugs and 29 percent report they were under the influence of alcohol at the time of their offense. Sixty percent of women in state prison were using drugs in the month before the offense. One-third of women in prison said they committed the offense to obtain money for drugs.[63]

- *Reestablishing relationships with children after incarceration is difficult.* Research shows that incarceration of a mother results in emotional, financial, and social suffering for children and that often mother-child relationships are beyond repair after a period of incarceration. It may be more difficult for mothers to have personal visits with their children while incarcerated because they are typically located in distant facilities—an average of 160 miles farther from their children than are incarcerated fathers.[64]

HOW ARE RELEASE DECISIONS MADE?

In the past, most prisoners were released after parole boards deemed them "ready." They would serve a portion of their sentence in prison and a portion in the community under parole supervision. The benefits of this method, in theory, were that release decisions were based on some assessment of individual risk, and that prisoners had an incentive to behave well and participate in programs while incarcerated. In the late 1970s and early 1980s, indeterminate sentencing and parole release fell out of favor among policymakers, ushering in significant policy changes. In the 1980s and 1990s, truth-in-sentencing laws were passed, functionally eliminating the role of the parole board for certain prisoners. As a result of these changes, there are now fewer prisoners released because of a parole board decision, more prisoners released "automatically" under mandatory release (with supervision to follow), and more prisoners whose sentences expire and are released without any supervision at all.

The term "parole" refers to two different matters:

- the decision made by a parole board to release a prisoner onto parole supervision, and

- the period of conditional supervision following a prison term.

The movement to abolish parole release resulted in significant reductions in the percentage of prison release decisions made by parole boards. The "truth-in-sentencing" movement also capped the portion of a sentence served in the community, typically to 15 percent of the original sentence. As a result, more prisoners are now returned to the community with less or no time under supervision, and with less consideration of "readiness" for release. A system of parole *supervision*, however, is still operational in some form in nearly all states.

During the past few decades, the importance of victim participation in parole release decisions has grown. In a recent study of state parole boards, a majority ranked the input of victims as a very important component of the decision-making process. As of 1991, 31 states allow victims to participate in parole board hearings, and an additional 4 states allow victims to attend the hearings. More than 90 percent of state parole boards provide information to victims on the status of the parole process.[69]

Under indeterminate sentencing practices, prisoners were released from prison to parole only after a parole board had deemed them "ready"—meaning, at least theoretically, they had been rehabilitated and/or had productive connections to the community, such as a job, a housing arrangement, and ties to family. Release to parole was positioned as a privilege to be earned. However, this system was increasingly criticized over the years as arbitrary, racially biased, and a politically expedient way to relieve prison overcrowding.[65] A series of sentencing reforms passed over the past two decades have diminished the role and power of parole boards to make individualized release decisions.

In addition, truth-in-sentencing laws were passed in the early 1980s and 1990s to reduce the discrepancy between the sentence imposed and the actual time individuals serve in prison. Forty states have enacted truth-in-sentencing laws requiring that violent offenders serve at least 50 percent of their sentences in prison; of these states, 27 and the District of Columbia require violent offenders to serve at least 85 percent of their sentences in prison.[66] These laws minimize the role of the parole board in making release decisions. As a result, fewer prisoners are now released because of a parole board decision.

As illustrated in table 2, in 1990, 39 percent of inmates were released as a result of a parole board decision. By 1998, the portion had dropped to 26 percent. Consequently, 40 percent of state inmates are now mandatorily released (1998 figures), up from 29 percent in 1990.

This development has implications for corrections management. Does the absence of a discretionary release process remove an incentive for good behavior? Does an automatic release process diminish the prisoner's incentive to find a stable residence or employment on the outside—the factors that traditionally influenced parole board decisions? Does a mandatory release policy decrease a correctional agency's commitment to developing links between an inmate's life in prison and his or her life outside prison? Does mandatory release remove the ability of a parole board to reconsider the risk posed by the individual, once his

Table 2. Inmate Release Decisions, 1990–98

| Year | Released to Supervision | | | Unconditional Releases | |
	Parole Board	Mandatory Release	Other Conditional	Expiration of Sentence	Other
1990	39.4%	28.8%	15.5%	12.7%	3.6%
1995	32.3%	39.0%	10.1%	14.5%	4.0%
1996	30.4%	38.0%	10.2%	16.7%	4.7%
1997	28.2%	39.7%	10.4%	16.8%	4.9%
1998	26.0%	40.4%	11.2%	18.7%	3.7%

Source: A. J. Beck, "State and Federal Prisoners Returning to the Community: Findings from the Bureau of Justice Statistics." Paper presented at the First Reentry Courts Initiative Cluster Meeting, April 13, 2000.

or her prison behavior has been observed? And, for states with policies granting victims' rights to participate in parole board hearings, what role do victims have in the release process?

In addition, more prisoners are serving their full term and therefore are released with no supervision at all. As shown in table 2, some 22 percent of prisoners were released "unconditionally" in 1998. The number of inmates released unconditionally has nearly doubled since 1990: More than 100,000 prisoners are now released unconditionally each year.[67] In most of these cases, prisoners have served their full term in prison (i.e., "maxed out" or "wrapped") and therefore face no time under parole or community supervision at the end of their sentence.

Figure 6. Sentenced Prisoners Released from State Prisons, by Conditional or Unconditional Release, 1977–98

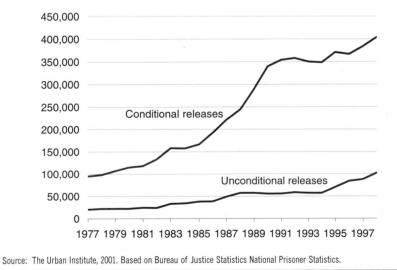

Source: The Urban Institute, 2001. Based on Bureau of Justice Statistics National Prisoner Statistics.

Definitions[68]

- *Determinate Sentencing*—A prison sentence with a fixed term of imprisonment that can be reduced by good-time or earned-time credits.

- *Indeterminate Sentence*—A prison sentence whose maximum or minimum term is established at the time of sentencing—but not a fixed term. Parole boards determine when to release individuals from prison.

- *Mandatory Release*—The release of an inmate from prison that is determined by statute or sentencing guidelines and is not decided by a panel or board.

- *Discretionary Release*—The release of an inmate from prison to supervision that is decided by a board or other authority.

- *Conditional Release*—The release of an inmate from prison to community supervision with a set of conditions for remaining on parole. Conditions can include regular reporting to a parole officer, drug testing, curfews, and other conditions. If the conditions are violated, the individual can be returned to prison or face another sanction in the community.

- *Unconditional Release*—The release of an inmate from prison where he is not under supervision of a community corrections agency and is not required to abide by special conditions (and therefore cannot be returned to prison without conviction for the commission of a new offense).

Typically, prisoners are released unconditionally for one of these three reasons: (1) they were convicted of a particularly violent crime, and may be less likely to be paroled;[70] (2) they behaved poorly in prison, thereby forfeiting possible good-time that would allow an earlier release; and (3) they were sentenced to relatively short terms, so parole or mandatory release may not be options.[71] For these prisoners, there are no additional obligations to report to a parole officer or to abide by certain conditions of release. Nationally, very little is known about the behavior and recidivism rates of prisoners released who are under criminal justice supervision compared with those who are not. This issue clearly warrants further examination.

Unconditional Releases

As illustrated in figure 7, the practice of releasing prisoners "unconditionally" varies widely by state. While some states do not release any prisoners without post-prison supervision, some release more than half of the state's prison population unconditionally.

Figure 7. Unconditional Releases as a Percentage of All Releases, by State, 1998

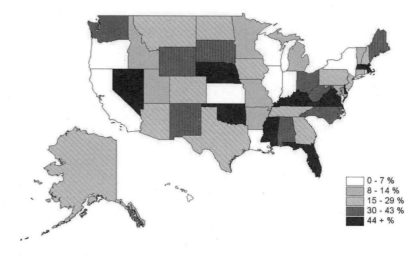

0 - 7 %
8 - 14 %
15 - 29 %
30 - 43 %
44 + %

Source: The Urban Institute, 2001. Based on Bureau of Justice Statistics National Prisoner Statistics.

HOW ARE PRISONERS PREPARED FOR RELEASE AND REINTEGRATION?

Given that nearly all prisoners will eventually be released back to the community—40 percent within the next 12 months—prison could be viewed as an opportunity to improve inmates' skills, treat their addictions, and prepare them generally for life on the outside. As discussed above, many prisoners have histories of substance abuse and addiction, mental and physical health problems, and low levels of job skills and education. There is some evidence that in-prison programs are cost-effective and beneficial in preparing inmates for life outside of prison. However, recent surveys indicate that relatively few inmates receive treatment or training while in prison.

Following a period of pessimism that characterized the "nothing works" sentiment of the 1970s, experts are increasingly, albeit cautiously, optimistic about the effectiveness of certain in-prison programs at changing behavior. While the quality and quantity of the available evidence varies widely according to the type of intervention, it does seem that certain treatment interventions— including cognitive skills, drug treatment, vocational training, educational, and other prison-based programs—are successful at reducing recidivism. These interventions are most effective when programs are matched to prisoner risks and needs, when they are well-managed, and when the intervention is supported through post-release supervision. While current studies cite only modest reductions in recidivism rates for participants, these small reductions can have significant aggregate impacts on criminal behavior in communities with high concentrations of returning prisoners.[72]

In addition to individual rehabilitative benefits, programming also may be beneficial to the internal management of correctional institutions.[73] Idle prisoners are more likely to cause trouble than other prisoners. According to research on the topic, some level of structured activity (education, job training, prison industry, or similar activities) is vital to running a safe and humane prison.[74]

Most prisoners do not participate in prison programs, however, and the rate of participation has dropped over the last decade. As shown in figure 8, about one-third of soon-to-be-released inmates reported they participated in vocational programs (27 percent) or educational programs (35 percent), down from 31 percent and 43 percent, respectively, in 1991.[75] These decreases in the participation rates are steeper than they appear, because smaller shares of bigger populations are involved—meaning significantly larger numbers of prisoners are being released without vocational and educational preparation.

Figure 8. Prisoners to be Released in the Next 12 Months: Percentage Participating in Prison Programs, 1991 and 1997

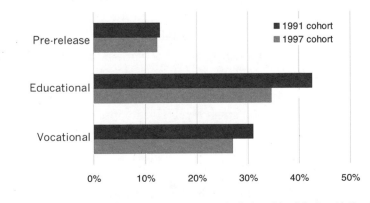

Source: J.P. Lynch and W.J. Sabol, "Prisoner Reentry in Perspective." Urban Institute *Crime Policy Report,* forthcoming.

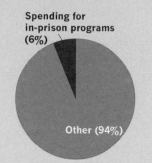

**Spending for
in-prison programs
(6%)**

Other (94%)

Further, although the majority of prison inmates enter prison with substance abuse problems, only 10 percent of state inmates in 1997 reported receiving professional substance abuse treatment, down from 25 percent in 1991.
Of the soon-to-be-released population, 18 percent of those with a substance
abuse problem received treatment while incarcerated.[76] In addition, an estimated 7 percent of the prison population report participating in prison industries, and 24 percent are altogether idle.[77] Participation of soon-to-be-released
inmates in the activities explicitly labeled "pre-release programs" remained stable
between 1991 and 1997, hovering at just 12 percent.[78]

In sum, the profile of the prison population reveals significant deficiencies
in human capital that reduce an individual's capacity to function and contribute to society. Many of these deficits are also associated with high rates of recidivism. The emerging research knowledge about effective prison programs
suggests that targeted investments in these interventions could produce public
safety benefits and increase social functioning overall. Ironically, the research
consensus comes at a time when a smaller share of prisoners seem to be receiving treatment and training than in the past.

THE MOMENT OF RELEASE

**The "moment of release" from prison, and the hours and days that
follow, may be quite pivotal to the transition back to community life.
There are multiple hurdles—many of a largely logistical nature—
that could be overcome relatively easily with appropriate planning.
Systematic attention to small but significant details, important at
the moment of release, such as the time of day prisoners are
released, whether they have identification, and arranging for
housing, treatment, jobs, and family reunification immediately upon
release could help ease their transition from prison to community.**

Following release from prison, inmates are moved directly from a very con-
trolled environment to a low level of supervision or complete freedom. They
may immediately be exposed to high-risk places, persons, and situations, and
few have developed relapse prevention skills during their incarceration to deal
with these risks. Prisoners facing release often report feeling anxious about reestablishing family ties, finding employment, and managing finances once they
return to their communities.[79] Indeed, even though the existence of "gate fe-
ver"—a syndrome defined by anxiety and irritability at the time of a prisoner's
release—is widely recognized among correctional workers, few empirical studies have investigated the issue. The little research that has been conducted
concludes that while very few prisoners ultimately find the experience of release debilitating, the heightened stress levels documented at the time of release reflect very real anxieties about successfully managing a return to the
outside world.[80]

The heightened stress levels among inmates associated with the moment
of release stem from anxieties about everyday problems—whether related to
interpersonal relationships or financial pressures—that did not exist for the

inmates while in prison. As previous studies have demonstrated, released offenders tend to cope with everyday problems in ineffective and sometimes destructive ways. In fact, research that has attempted to measure the coping process has shown that some offenders are unable to successfully recognize and deal with problem situations, leading to increased stress levels and rash, often criminal reactions.[83]

There has been little systematic attention, by corrections agencies or communities, on ways to reduce the risks associated with the moment of release. Many practices may in fact heighten the anxiety prisoners have about successfully returning to the outside world. Some may even increase the risk of failure.

Most prisoners are released with little more than a bus ticket and a nominal amount of spending money. Some states provide bus tickets to return ex-prisoners to their destination (often the county of sentencing), but only half report making any transportation arrangements. For those states that do provide funds, the amount ranges from about $25 to $200. About one-third of all departments of corrections report that they do not provide any funds upon release.[84]

Prisoners are often returned to their home community at odd hours of the night, making it difficult for them to connect with family and service providers during the critical first few hours following release. Prisoners are often returned home without the important pieces of identification necessary to obtain jobs, get access to substance abuse treatment, or apply for public assistance. For example, some former prisoners experience delays in entering drug treatment because they do not have Medicaid.[85] Finally, those who are released may not fully understand the criminal justice system requirements they need to fulfill. In a survey of all states conducted in 2000 by the American Correctional Association, two-thirds reported that they do not provide any documentation or reporting instructions to inmates upon release.[86]

Thus, the "moment of release" presents opportunities for policy innovation and attention—to develop strategies that build a short-term bridge during this immediate transition period. Currently, released prisoners encounter few resources to help them secure employment, access substance-abuse treatment, and reestablish family and community ties. The combination of these pre-release preparations coupled with follow-up on the outside (via parole, nonprofit community organizations, faith institutions, family, or friends) might reduce the risk of recidivism or drug relapse and improve the odds of successful reintegration after release.

Work Release

Since the early 1920s, work-release programs have provided soon-to-be-released prisoners with the skills and training necessary to secure employment. These programs allow for selected prisoners to work in the community, returning to their correctional facilities during non-working hours. Work-release programs provide prisoners with income that may be used to build up savings for when they are eventually released, to help reimburse the state for portions of their confinement costs, and to help pay for victim restitution or make child support payments.

While extremely popular in the 1970s, today, only about one-third of prisons operate work-release programs and fewer than 3 percent of all inmates participate in them. Certain highly publicized work-release failures, combined with shrinking funding and a general philosophical move away from the ideal of rehabilitation, have contributed to the decline of such programs.

However, some states such as Washington maintain high levels of funding and other means of support for its work-release program. Two National Institute of Justice-sponsored evaluations of Washington's program found it relatively successful. Almost 40 percent of all prisoners released in Washington went through a work-release program in 1990, and fewer than 5 percent of these prisoners committed new crimes while in the program. Ninety-nine percent of these crimes were less serious property offenses. Fifty-six percent of all program enrollees were judged successful in work release. Results from a follow-up study tracking recidivism among former work-release participants were also positive, but to a lesser degree: Researchers found that within one year 22 percent of work-release participants had been rearrested, compared with 30 percent of ex-prisoners who had not participated in the program.[87]

The First Month Out: Post-Incarceration Experiences in New York City[88]

In 1999, the Vera Institute of Justice followed a group of 49 adults released from New York state prisons and city jails for 30 days, interviewing them on seven separate occasions to learn about the major challenges facing returning prisoners during this period. The study sought to gain insight into returning prisoners' expectations, the release experience, reunions with family and friends, attempts to find work, and parole supervision experiences. This study indicates that the initial period following release from prison is critical. Although the small sample size limits the broader applicability of the findings, the patterns found can help enrich our understanding of the experience and challenges of reentry and reintegration from the perspective of the returning prisoner.

This study documented a few key hurdles to successful reintegration—namely, finding a job, finding housing, and getting access to needed health care services. Most returning prisoners who found a job within the first month following their release were either re-hired by former employers or had help from family or friends. Relatively few found new jobs on their own, often because they lacked the skills to conduct an effective job search or could not find employers who would hire ex-offenders. Few parolees reported receiving help from their parole officers. In fact, strong family involvement or support was an important indicator of successful reintegration across the board. Returning prisoners who indicated that their families or friends were supportive of their efforts to rebuild their lives had lower levels of drug use, greater likelihood of finding a job, and less continued criminal activity. Most people lived with their families following their release, indicating some level of support. Those who went to homeless shelters were seven times as likely to abscond from parole.

Vera also found that the moment of release is an important opportunity for starting out on the right path. The majority of people interviewed at the time of their release returned to their communities alone. Only a small number of returning prisoners were met by family members, friends, or social service representatives. Further, some prisoners were released without basic identification, hindering their efforts to apply for public assistance or drug treatment. Others experienced delays in getting drug treatment because they did not have Medicaid or could not obtain a referral to a treatment program. In fact, lack of Medicaid—a process that could begin before release—was the biggest obstacle to accessing treatment following release. None of the individuals who relapsed attended treatment regularly.

POST-RELEASE SUPERVISION

Although fewer release decisions are being made by parole boards, the great majority of returning prisoners are subject to some period of post-prison supervision in the community. Of the more than half-million state prisoners released last year, more than three-fourths were released to some kind of post-prison supervision, most frequently "parole." Growing incarceration and release rates over the last two decades have resulted in a growing parolee population, and resources have not kept pace with those increases. Caseloads are higher, per capita spending is lower, and services have diminished. We know little about parole effectiveness, but what we do know suggests that surveillance alone does not work. Supervision strategies that include some level of treatment or a rehabilitation component in combination with surveillance techniques have been shown to reduce recidivism.

The majority of prisoners—78 percent—are released from prison onto some type of conditional supervision status.[89] Individuals released to parole supervision serve an average of just under two years in their states.[90] There are 713,000 individuals now on parole (or another form of conditional release),[91] up from 220,000 in 1980.[92] The increase in the prison population has had the predictable impact of increasing the parole population, without proportionate increases in resources. This translates into bigger caseloads for parole officers. In the 1970s, the average parole officer supervised a caseload of 45 parolees. Today, most officers are responsible for about 70 parolees—about twice as high as is considered ideal.[93] At the same time, per capita spending per parolee has decreased nationally—from more than $11,000 per year in 1985 to about $9,500 in 1998.[94]

These limited resources often translate into only nominal supervision. More than 80 percent of parolees are supervised on "regular" caseloads—each meeting with a parole officer for about 15 minutes, once or twice a month.[95] An additional 8 percent of parolees (or more than 56,000 individuals in 1998) are classified on "abscond" status at any given time, meaning they cannot be found and have no contact with their parole officer.[96] In California, 18 to 20 percent of parolees are on abscond status.[97] Because supervisory agencies have lost touch with this group of released prisoners, we have little data about their behavior.

Conditions of parole vary widely by jurisdiction, but they typically include abstinence from drugs, maintaining employment, observing curfews, and staying away from certain high-risk places and persons. Enforcement of those conditions varies as well, but it may include home visits, drug testing, and electronic monitoring. A few states are experimenting with Global Positioning System satellites, where individuals' movements are tracked 24 hours a day. New surveillance technologies such as these have made supervision—at least the monitoring aspect—more efficient, but they raise important civil liberties issues as well.

Unfortunately, there is little research that examines the relationship between parole supervision and deterrence or rehabilitation. We do know that supervision strategies that simply increase the level of supervision, such as intensive community supervision, increased drug testing, and home confinement, have not been found to reduce reoffending. Rather, enhanced supervision involves increased surveillance that increases the likelihood of *detecting* technical violations.[98] If noncompliance with technical conditions of release signaled patterns of criminal behavior among individuals, then returning them to incarceration might prevent future crime. However, research on the issue has shown no support for the argument that violating parolees on technical conditions suppresses new criminal arrests.[99] Accordingly, there is no solid evidence to support the conclusion that solely increasing parole supervision will result in fewer crimes.

At the same time, supervision strategies that include some level of rehabilitation or treatment in combination with surveillance techniques have been shown to reduce recidivism. According to the research literature, a treatment component is important to changing behavior and reducing crime.[100]

On the whole, services for this population have diminished. More resources have gone into building new prison beds, making fewer funds available for investing in services. As discussed in the "communities" section at the end of this report, there is a large gap between the needs and availability of services around

Reinventing Probation: Lessons for Parole?

One approach is currently being explored under the heading "reinventing probation." Spearheaded by the Reinventing Probation Council—a group of experienced and innovative probation practitioners (in collaboration with the Manhattan Institute)—this approach builds on the community policing model and involves place-based supervision strategies and partnerships among law enforcement agencies, community residents and organizations, and other public and private organizations. Policies under this rubric include proactive, problem-solving practices intended to prevent, control, and reduce crime and to repair harm to the victim and the community. Though the focus of the model is probation, the strategies are applicable to parole and reentry.

In the Council's most recent monograph, *Transforming Probation Through Leadership: The "Broken Windows" Model*, the authors describe a new strategy that involves

- placing public safety first;
- supervising individuals in the neighborhood;
- allocating resources where they are needed most;
- enforcing probation conditions and responding quickly to violations to deter behavior;
- developing partners in the community;
- establishing performance-based initiatives; and
- cultivating strong leadership.[101]

The question for policymakers is how to use probation and parole conditions, monitoring strategies, and graduated sanctions to help prisoners make a successful transition into the community and to deter criminal activity. To what extent could the combination of place-based strategies, individualized case plans based on empirically derived risk/needs instruments, and graduated responses to failure improve supervision outcomes?

issues such as substance abuse, mental health, and housing.

Given the high rates of reoffending within this population, there seems to be an important opportunity to supervise parolees—particularly the high-risk individuals—by combining treatment and surveillance to prevent future crimes.

PAROLE VIOLATIONS

More parolees are returning to prison than ever before, both for technical violations and for committing new offenses. In 1980, parole violators constituted 18 percent of prison admissions. Parole violators now account for one-third of prison admissions nationally. Of the parole violators returned to prison, nearly one-third were returned for a new conviction and two-thirds for a technical violation. There is little research on the nature of technical violations or the parole revocation process itself, nor do we know the impact of the increasing numbers of parole revocations and reincarceration on public safety.

If parolees fail to meet their conditions of supervision or are convicted for a new crime, their parole can be revoked and they can be returned to prison. That is happening more frequently. In 1984, 70 percent of parolees successfully completed their parole term. By 1998, that number had dropped to 45 percent. Put another way, in 1998 nearly half of all parolees (42 percent) were returned to prison, translating to some 206,000 parole violators who were returned that year.[102] Parole violators as a share of prison admissions have doubled since the 1980s. In 1980, parole violators constituted 18 percent of prison admissions; they now represent a full one-third of all prison admissions.[103]

Unfortunately, the administrative recording of parole violations does not tell us much about the underlying behavior of the parolee. Of the parole violators returned to prison, nearly one-third were returned for a new conviction and two-thirds for a technical violation.[104] However, although many violations are formally recorded as "technical," they may not be crime-free in nature. Often technical violators are actually arrested (but not tried for) a new crime while under parole supervision. For example, 43 percent of the "technical" violators in 1991 reported having been arrested for a new crime at least once while on parole.[105] For policy and practice, it is important that we better understand the actual reasons behind parole violations and revocations.

It is unclear why parole failures are higher now than in the past. It may be a function of better monitoring techniques and technologies that make it easier to detect violations such as drug use and missed curfews. It is also possible that technical violations are being used as a tool for managing increasingly large caseloads. Parole revocation may be an expression of tough-on-crime sentiment in some jurisdictions, or perhaps more individuals are actually committing crimes while on parole. This failure rate may also reflect cutbacks in preparation for reentry, such as in-prison and community-based treatment, job training, and education. Importantly, it is not clear whether supervision agencies are

Between 1990 and 1998, there has been a 54 percent increase in the number of individuals returned to prison for a parole violation. Drug offenders account for more than half of this increase.[106]

Policy-Driven Responses to Parole Violations

Beginning in 1998, the National Institute of Corrections provided funding to 19 paroling authorities and probation agencies to test policy-driven responses to technical parole violations. A report by the Center for Effective Public Policy documents significant variation in parole practices, both across these states and across localities within states. In many jurisdictions, probation and parole officers have enormous discretion and relatively little guidance from formal policy.[107]

Through this effort, state parole administrators began to review the decisions (both formal and informal) that led to parole violations. Many jurisdictions have since formulated new responses to technical violations, ranging from violation guidelines designed to keep individuals on parole in lieu of incarceration to new alternatives to incarceration.[108]

efficiently identifying the highest-risk parolees and preventing new crimes or inefficiently returning individuals to the correctional system—at high cost to state taxpayers without clear crime control benefits.

As an alternative to reincarceration, some states—still a minority—use intermediate sanctions for violations, such as residential treatment, community service, electronic monitoring, curfew, increased supervision level, loss of travel privileges, counseling, increased drug/alcohol testing, or reprimand by officer or supervisor. Structured sanctions provide a graduated response, with reincarceration as the most severe sanction. The hypothesis here is that immediate, intermediate sanctions could increase the certainty of punishment, change offender behavior, and reduce returns to prison, while reserving prison beds for violent individuals. Limited evidence suggests that a system of graduated sanctions may be more effective in reducing recidivism than simply returning parole violators to prison. Certainty of sanctions appears to be highly correlated with positive changes in individual behavior. This certainty is based on consistent application of a sanctioning schedule and intense monitoring of behaviors where individuals are not able to have infractions go undetected, thereby reinforcing the unwanted behavior.

Despite the significant fiscal and public safety implications, parole has received remarkably little attention from policymakers, practitioners, or researchers. Research could shed light on the costs associated with the growing number of parole violators, the nature of technical violations, the parole revocation process, and the impact of parole policies on preventing new crimes. Imposing rationality on a process that is little understood even by those in the criminal justice system can result in tremendous benefits. In this view, the prison funding now spent on the increasing admissions of technical violators could be made available for strengthening or creating community corrections systems or funds for other areas of government.

Figure 9. Parole Violators as a Percentage of All Prison Admissions, by State, 1998

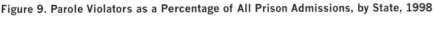

	7 - 18 %
	19 - 31 %
	32 - 44 %
	45 + %
	No Data

Source: The Urban Institute, 2001. Based on Bureau of Justice Statistics National Prisoner Statistics.

Fiscal Implications of Technical Violators

In California, where approximately 120,000 people are on parole, some 70,000 violate their conditions of parole each year. According to analysis by Michael Jacobson, professor at John Jay College of Criminal Justice and an Open Society Institute Fellow, the cost to California is almost $900 million annually, given that the average length of stay is about five months per violator. Jacobson estimates that if California "only" technically violated 35,000 of its parolees, it would save almost $500 million annually in corrections expenditures. If half of that money were reinvested into community corrections programs to create alternative programming for technical violators (day centers, intensive supervision with electronic bracelets, etc.), then parole officers would have far more options than short stays in prison.

Many states are experiencing similar impacts of technical parole and probation violators on correctional systems and budgets. Even in a small state like Iowa, technical violations are one of the primary drivers of its correctional system population. With almost 1,200 technical probation violators spending an average of between one-and-a-half and two years in prison, almost 25 percent of Iowa's prison population is comprised of technical violators.

Just as there is wide variation across the states in supervision practices, we see enormous variation in parole revocation rates. Figure 9 illustrates these differences through the percentage of prison admissions who are parole violators. In 1998, for example, 65 percent of the individuals admitted to California's prisons were parole violators, while in Florida, parole violators accounted for just 12 percent of new admissions. In Pennsylvania, parole violations account for 33 percent—just under the national average.[109]

Challenges for Prisoner Reentry

Given the high prevalence of substance abuse, mental illness, infectious disease, unemployment, and even homelessness among returning prisoners, it is important to explore the role of these factors in successful reentry and reintegration. To the extent that these issues present serious barriers to transitioning prisoners, they also present serious risks to the communities to which large numbers of prisoners return. It is important to note how little we know about how these problems overlap. The difficulties faced in dual and triple diagnosis (for substance abuse, mental illness, and HIV infection, for example) are particularly acute, and the associated service needs are even more complex and challenging. This section examines the role of substance abuse, health, employment, and housing in post-prison adjustment and points to programmatic and policy strategies that may reduce the likelihood of future offending.

SUBSTANCE ABUSE

Substance abuse among prisoners presents significant challenges to the reentry process. Studies have found that while most prisoners have a history of drug or alcohol abuse, only a small share receive treatment while incarcerated and upon release. Importantly, treatment has been shown to reduce drug use and criminal activity, particularly when in-prison treatment is combined with treatment in the community. In this section, we discuss the prevalence of substance abuse among returning prisoners, the effectiveness of treatment, and the implications of both on reentry.

Eighty percent of the state prison population report a history of drug and/or alcohol use,[110] including 74 percent of those expected to be released within the next 12 months.[111] In fact, more than half of state prisoners report that they were using drugs or alcohol when they committed the offense that led to their incarceration.[112]

The movement from confinement in prison to liberty on the street poses unique hazards for prisoners with a history of substance abuse. Rates of relapse following release from prison are strikingly high in the absence of treatment. For example, an estimated two-thirds of untreated heroin abusers resume their heroin/cocaine use and patterns of criminal behavior within three months of their release.[113] The extent to which substance abuse problems are treated prior to and following release from prison has significant implications on the outcomes of returning prisoners.

Several studies have found that drug treatment can be a beneficial and cost-effective way to reduce both substance abuse and criminal activity.[114] Two common treatment modalities typically used with correctional populations and found to have positive effects are cognitive behavioral interventions and in-prison therapeutic communities. In the last 15 years, there has been general agreement among researchers that cognitive-behavioral programs can reduce recidivism among the general offender population. These programs, based on social learning theory, assume that criminal behavior is learned and therefore they focus on improving interpersonal and coping skills.[115] Although research has found that such programs can reduce criminal recidivism, they also have been found to be less effective among individuals below the age of 25 and among those whose offenses involved property and nonviolent robbery.[116] In fact, cognitive, skill-building programs were most effective with individuals on probation.

Another common approach found to have positive effects on relapse and recidivism is in-prison residential treatment. Therapeutic communities or residential treatment typically lasts 6 to 12 months and often involves separating the participants from the general prison population. Several studies have found that these programs can reduce drug use following release from prison. For instance, inmates who participated in residential treatment programs during incarceration had criminal recidivism rates between 9 and 18 percent lower and drug relapse rates between 15 and 35 percent lower than those who received no treatment in prison.[117] An ongoing evaluation of a residential drug treatment program within the Federal Bureau of Prisons has found reduced recidivism and relapse rates among treated inmates six months following release. Specifically, inmates who completed the residential treatment program were 73 percent less likely to be rearrested than untreated inmates. Likewise, treated inmates were also 44 percent less likely than untreated offenders to use drugs within the first six months following release.[118]

In-prison drug treatment has also been associated with significantly reduced use of injection drugs, reduced income from crime, fewer prison returns, and fewer hospital stays for drug and alcohol problems.[119] However, the most successful outcomes were found among those who participated in both in-prison treatment and community treatment during the period of post-release supervision.[120] There are also indications that the longer the treatment intervention—at least 90 days—the more successful it will be in reducing relapse.[121] (Research also shows that the presence of criminal justice supervision increases the likelihood that an individual will stay in treatment beyond the 90-day mark.)

Although more than three-quarters of state inmates indicate a history of drug and/or alcohol use, in-prison treatment is not readily available to most of those who need it. In fact, only 10 percent of state inmates in 1997 reported receiving formal substance abuse treatment, down from 25 percent in 1991.[123] Of the soon-to-be-released prisoners (in 1997) who were using drugs in the month before their incarceration, only 18 percent had received treatment since they were admitted to prison.[124]

Alcohol abuse is also a significant and under-addressed problem for prisoners. Among violent offenders in state prison, some 38 percent had been drinking at the time of their offense, yet only 18 percent of this group received in-prison treatment.[125] Of those inmates who were alcohol-dependent at the time of their incarceration, slightly more than one-fifth received in-prison treatment.[126]

The positive effects of in-prison treatment have been found to be most effective when combined with community-based aftercare. One study of in-prison treatment combined with aftercare found a 28 percent reduction in criminal recidivism and a 62 percent reduction in drug use.[127] In a world of limited resources, attention should be paid to *when* treatment is made available during the period of incarceration. Participation in a treatment program may be most effective for prisoners who are nearing the end of their term and preparing to be released back into society. It also suggests that links to and participation in community-based care following in-prison treatment are warranted.

Research on substance abuse has also found that "addiction is a brain disease."[128] The experience of a prisoner returning to his old neighborhood and friends places him at high risk for relapse, in part because the familiar places and people may act as a trigger to his brain and heighten cravings. Helping to smooth this transition—through connections to community-based treatment, perhaps immediately upon release—could reduce the likelihood of recidivism and the resumption of drug use.

PHYSICAL AND MENTAL HEALTH

The prevalence of major mental disorders and chronic and infectious disease is many times greater among the prison population than among the general population.[129] While most individuals receive needed health care services in prison, access to mental health services is more limited, and follow-up to community-based care is lacking. There is an opportunity to maximize the investment in prison health care by linking those services to treatment in the community. Such links would also reduce public health and public safety risks.

Social and policy shifts have resulted in an inmate population with relatively high rates of serious physical and mental health problems. The 1980s and 1990s were marked by increased drug use, tougher sentencing policies, and enhanced enforcement, resulting in a larger number of incarcerated drug offenders. One quarter of all state and federal inmates reportedly have histories of injection drug use and a higher risk of infectious disease.[130] Also, the passage of mandatory minimum and truth-in-sentencing reforms has resulted in an older inmate population.[131] In inmate surveys, older prisoners were more likely to report medical problems than younger inmates. Finally, following the widespread

Treatment is Cost-Effective

A 1997 RAND study looked at the relative benefits of spending an additional $1 million to cut drug consumption and related drug crime via different policy interventions. Researchers concluded that spending funds to reduce drug consumption through treatment rather than incarceration would reduce serious crimes 15 times more effectively.[132] Another study in California reported savings from treatment of $1.5 billion over 18 months, with the largest savings coming from reductions in crime.[133] The study estimated that for every $1 spent on treatment, approximately $7 could be gained in future savings.

deinstitutionalization of mentally ill persons from state psychiatric hospitals in the 1960s and 1970s, more of these individuals are now involved in the criminal justice system.[135] In fact, 16 percent of state inmates report a mental condition or an overnight stay in a psychiatric hospital.[136]

A large number of people carrying communicable diseases pass through correctional facilities each year. As shown in table 4, released prisoners account for a significant share of the total population who are infected with HIV or AIDS, hepatitis B and C, and tuberculosis. During 1997, between 20 and 26 percent of the nation's individuals living with HIV or AIDS, 29 to 32 percent of the people with hepatitis C, and 38 percent of those with tuberculosis were released from a correctional facility (prison or jail).

Table 4. Percentage of Total Burden of Infectious Disease Among People Passing Through Correctional Facilities, 1997

Condition	Est. number of releasees with condition, 1997	Total number in U.S. population with condition	Releasees with condition as percentage of total population with condition
AIDS	39,000	247,000	16%
HIV Infection	112,000–158,000	503,000	22–31%
Total HIV/AIDS	151,000–197,000	750,000	20–26%
Hepatitis B Infection	155,000	1–1.25 million	12–16%
Hepatitis C Infection	1.3–1.4 million	4.5 million	29–32%
Tuberculosis Disease	12,000	32,000	38%

Source: T.M. Hammett, "Health-Related Issues in Prisoner Reentry to the Community." Paper presented at the Reentry Roundtable, Washington, D.C., Oct. 12–13, 2000.

Considering only the prison population, we see substantially higher rates of serious infectious disease than in the general population. For instance, the overall rate of confirmed AIDS cases among inmates was five times the rate found among the general population (0.55 percent versus 0.10 percent, respectively).[137] In 1997, 2.2 percent of state prisoners tested HIV positive, a rate five to seven times greater than that in the general population. And 18 percent of the inmate population were infected with hepatitis C, nine to ten times the rate of the general population.[138]

These high infection rates present an enormous public health opportunity. Treatment regimens that begin in prison and continue upon release could have significant public health benefits and could reduce future costs of more expensive interventions and treatment of additional individuals.[139] Interestingly, a period of incarceration often has positive consequences for the physical health status of a prisoner—in part because adequate health care is constitutionally

State correctional agencies spend an average of 10 percent of their budgets on inmate health services, according to survey results reported in the *Correctional Compendium.*[134]

required, but also because the food and the living environment are more conducive to better health outcomes than many situations in the community.[140] Inmates typically have limited access to health care services before they arrive at a correctional facility. Once incarcerated, they have greater access to medical care than persons with similar sociodemographic characteristics.[141]

A survey of state inmates found that 80 percent reported receiving a medical exam since they were admitted to prison. More than half (nearly 60 percent) reported being checked to see if they were sick, injured, or intoxicated at the time of admission, and most (82 percent) were asked about their medical histories. Of those who reported a medical problem since admission, 91 percent reported visiting a health care professional about it.[142]

While access to in-prison health care services may be readily available, continued adherence to treatment regimens following release is a critical public health issue, especially for diseases such as HIV and tuberculosis. Although most state and federal prison systems provide some discharge planning for HIV-infected inmates, those services vary widely in quality.[143] For example, three-quarters of prison systems make referrals for HIV treatment/medications, Medicaid benefits, or sexually transmitted disease treatment. However, fewer than one-third of the correctional facilities report actually making appointments for releasees with specific treatment providers.[144] Even providing appointments, while an important first step, does not ensure that the person receives services. Another important barrier is the time it takes for many returning inmates to finalize their enrollment in various benefit programs.[145]

The extent of mental health disorders is also relatively high. While estimating the prevalence of mental illness among the inmate population is difficult, we know that serious mental health disorders such as schizophrenia/psychosis, major depression, bipolar disorder, and post-traumatic stress disorder are more common among prisoners than the general population.[146] Rates of mental illness among incarcerated individuals are at least twice (some estimates range as high as four times) as high as the rates in the overall U.S. population.[147] It is estimated that between 8 and 16 percent of the prison population have at least one serious mental disorder and are in need of psychiatric services.[148]

More than half (60 percent) of mentally ill state inmates have reportedly received some form of mental health treatment during their period of incarceration.[149] Of these, half said they had taken prescription medication and 44 percent had received counseling services. Ensuring the successful reintegration of ex-prisoners with mental disorders depends, at least in part, on the availability of treatment in the community. Unfortunately, several studies have concluded that parole agencies are unable to effectively identify and address the needs of mentally ill parolees. A national survey of parole administrators indicated that fewer than a quarter provide special programs for parolees with mental illness.[150]

A closer look at this population of inmates reveals that they are at high risk on several fronts. A significant number have dual diagnoses of mental health and substance abuse issues.[151] More than one-third of mentally ill state inmates indicated a history of alcohol dependence, and nearly six in ten indicated that

Studies of adherence to tuberculosis treatment after release have found adherence to be low. However, after a New York City health department program offered incentives for follow-up appointments, appearances at those appointments increased from less than 20 percent to 92 percent.[152]

they were under the influence of alcohol or drugs while committing their current offense. This combination is a strong predictor of recidivism.[153] Mentally ill inmates also reported longer criminal histories than other inmates.[154] More than half (52 percent) reported three or more prior offenses. Likewise, among repeat offenders, mentally ill inmates were more likely to have a current or past sentence for a violent offense. Finally, mentally ill prisoners were more likely to have been homeless before incarceration and on average are expected to serve 15 months longer in prison than other inmates.[155]

In sum, in-prison health systems have become significant providers of physical and mental health services to a population of poor and unhealthy persons. In-prison treatment is important, but as was noted with regard to substance abuse services, the critical point for reentry management is to link prison-based services with community-based services.

Models for Providing Mental Health Services to Parolees[156]

Specialized services for parolees with mental illness may help reduce recidivism and ensure a more successful reintegration. A number of jurisdictions have implemented specialized units or programs that are staffed by officers with educational backgrounds and experience working with mentally ill populations. Specialization is needed to identify and address the multiple and complex issues facing mentally ill returning prisoners, who often are struggling with substance abuse, developmental disabilities, poor physical health, homelessness, and little social support.

For example, the California Department of Corrections provides specialized services for mentally ill parolees through five Parolee Outpatient Clinics in San Diego, Los Angeles, San Francisco, Sacramento, and Fresno. The clinics serve only mentally ill parolees and are staffed by licensed psychiatrists and psychologists. While these clinics served nearly 9,000 mentally ill parolees in 1998, estimates suggest that half of those in need of service live outside the catchment area and are not receiving services.

California also operates a community-based Conditional Release Program for seriously mentally ill inmates who are transferred from prisons, to state hospitals, and then to outpatient psychiatric programs as a condition of parole. Eligible participants must have been in mental health treatment in prison for 90 days or more during the past year and assessed as substantial public safety risks. Following completion of treatment services in a hospital facility, parolees are released to community supervision where they continue to receive mental health care. Studies show that treatment participants are four times less likely to reoffend than similar parolees who do not go through the program—a success rate comparable to that of parolees in similar programs in New York and Oregon.

Another example is the Hampden County, Mass., Public Health Model for Corrections. Working with a jail population, the program provides intensive screening to inmates on arrival, education on health issues throughout their incarceration, and access to regular long-term health care during their jail stay and after release. The program, which began in 1992 with an HIV-awareness course, now provides comprehensive medical services to inmates through contractual agreements with established nonprofit community health centers. Each inmate is assigned to a physician and caseworker, and these assignments provide continuous long-term health care to an inmate during his or her stay and after release. The effects of the program are impressive: 100 percent of Hampden County jail inmates are provided with a complete physical during their stay in jail, and 90 percent of the inmates keep medical appointments after they have been released back into the community. The Hampden County recidivism rate stands at 9 percent, far lower than recidivism rates for comparable correctional facilities.[157]

EMPLOYABILITY AND WORKFORCE PARTICIPATION

There is a complex relationship between crime and employment. Having a legitimate job lessens the chances of reoffending following release from prison. Also, the higher the wages, the less likely it is that returning prisoners will return to crime.[158] However, studies also show that released prisoners confront a diminished prospect for stable employment and decent wages throughout their lifetimes. Job training and placement programs show promise in connecting ex-prisoners to work, thereby reducing their likelihood of further offending. Yet, fewer inmates are receiving in-prison vocational training than in the past and fewer still have access to transitional programs that help connect them to jobs in the community.

The ability to find a stable and adequate source of income upon release from prison is an important factor in an individual's transition from prison back to the community. Studies have shown that having a job with decent wages is associated with lower rates of reoffending. Put another way, reductions in wages are likely to lead to increases in illegal earnings and criminal activity. According to one estimate, a 10 percent decrease in an individual's wages is associated with 10 to 20 percent increase in his or her criminal activity and the likelihood of incarceration.[159]

Many offenders were connected to the world of legitimate work prior to incarceration and presumably want to find legal and stable employment following their release. Three-quarters of state inmates reportedly held a job just before their incarceration and, of those, just over half were employed full time.[160] Therefore, they must have had some skills and connections to mainstream work. It is no surprise, however, that released prisoners confront a diminished prospect for stable employment and decent wages throughout their lifetimes.

There are several reasons why incarceration reduces the employability and subsequent earning potential of released inmates. First, the stigma attached to incarceration makes it difficult for ex-prisoners to be hired. Employers are reluctant to hire individuals with a criminal record, because it signals that they may not be trustworthy.[161] A survey of employers in five major cities across the country revealed that two-thirds of all employers indicated they would not knowingly hire an ex-offender and at least one-third checked the criminal histories of their most recently hired employees.[162]

Returning inmates are also banned from working in certain fields. At least six states (Alabama, Delaware, Iowa, Mississippi, Rhode Island, and South Carolina) permanently bar ex-offenders from public employment.[163] Most states also impose restrictions on hiring ex-offenders for particular professions including law, real estate, medicine, nursing, physical therapy, and education.[164]

Additionally, time out of the labor market interrupts individuals' job experience and prevents them from building important employment skills. During the prison experience, they also become exposed to a prison culture that frequently serves to strengthen links to gangs and the criminal world in general.[165] Advancing in the legitimate labor market is a product of learning through new experiences and opportunities. The same is true for involvement in criminal activity for profit. Several studies looking at the impact of incarceration on future employment have concluded that as time spent in prison increases (net of other background factors) the likelihood of participating in the legal economy decreases.[166]

For all of these reasons, ex-prisoners have difficulty securing employment. While there are no national statistics about unemployment and underemployment among parolees, data from California are suggestive. In the early 1990s, only 21 percent of the parolee population in that state had full-time jobs.[167] When returning prisoners do secure jobs, they tend to earn less than individuals with similar background characteristics who have not been incarcerated. One researcher estimates the "wage penalty" of incarceration at about 10 to 20 percent.[168] Moreover, on average ex-inmates experience no real wage increases through their twenties and thirties, in sharp contrast to never-incarcerated young men whose wages grow rapidly through this period.[169]

The time of incarceration could be viewed as an opportunity to build skills and prepare for placement at a future job. The evaluation literature provides mixed support on the effectiveness of job training programs for offenders. Some studies have concluded that it is difficult to improve an individual's employment prospects and earnings, particularly if they have become "embedded in criminal activity."[170]

However, a more recent review of in-prison vocation and work programs provides a more optimistic outlook. There is some evidence that involvement in job training and placement programs can lead to employment and lower recidivism. On average, participants in vocational programs were more likely to be employed following release and to have a recidivism rate 20 percent lower than nonparticipants.[171] Although the current body of research does not provide enough evidence to support a definitive assertion that these programs "work"—because evaluations with positive findings have been methodologically weak—it does suggest that vocational programs may reduce recidivism for some motivated individuals.[172]

The most effective programs are those aimed at released prisoners in their mid-twenties or older. Specifically, a review of several studies indicates that work programs had a significant impact on the employment outcomes and recidivism rates of males who were over the age of 26.[173] These individuals may be more motivated than younger offenders to change their lifestyle and connections to crime. The fact that 80 percent of the prison population are 25 or older argues for more vocational training for a larger share of prisoners.

Studies also suggest that it is not enough to attempt to improve an individual's human capital. It is also important to address changes in motivation and lifestyle away from criminal activity to positive engagement in the community. This takes time, it is more complicated than teaching marketable skills, and it may mean reestablishing connections with organizations in the community.

One reason cited for why job training has not been more effective in reducing recidivism is the general lack of job placement assistance and other follow-up after release from prison. Programs such as the Safer Foundation, the

In 1997, fewer than one-third of soon-to-be-released state prisoners reported participating in vocational programs, down slightly from 1991.[174] Only 7 percent of the prison population participated in prison industries.[175]

Center for Employment Opportunities, and Re-Integration of Offenders (Project RIO) work to not only improve individuals' job skills but also to improve job readiness, provide case management for other services, place former prisoners in jobs, and continue to work with them for a follow-up period. This follow-up period may be particularly important for employers, who indicate a willingness to hire ex-prisoners if a third-party intermediary or case manager is available to work with the new hire to help avert problems.[176] Programs such as these, working within departments of correction or operating as community-based organizations, offer promise in connecting ex-prisoners to full-time employment, and lowering levels of criminal activity and substance abuse.

Job Placement Programs for Returning Prisoners

Opportunity to Succeed (OPTS) is a multi-site program designed to provide comprehensive aftercare services to felony offenders (parolees and probationers) who have alcohol and drug offense histories. In addition to services that deal with substance abuse, housing, family strengthening, health, and mental health issues, services are available to assist clients in finding and maintaining employment. OPTS is successful in helping clients attain full-time employment. An Urban Institute evaluation showed that OPTS clients demonstrated significantly longer periods of full-time employment than did control groups. OPTS clients who did find full-time employment showed lower rates of recidivism than those who did not.[182]

The **Center for Employment Opportunities (CEO)** is a New York City nonprofit organization that helps ex-offenders prepare for, locate, and retain jobs. The program offers day-labor assignments to provide structure in participants' lives and to develop good work habits. Participants are paid at the end of each day to provide them with immediate spending money, reinforce their dependability, and improve their self-esteem. CEO offers ongoing services to placed individuals for at least six months after placement. About 70 percent of participants find full-time employment within two to three months, and most jobs pay more than minimum wage and provide fringe benefits. Approximately three-fourths of participants are still employed at the same job after one month and about half are still at the same job after six months.[183]

Re-Integration of Offenders (Project RIO) in Texas provides job preparation services to inmates while they are still incarcerated in state prisons, giving them a head start on post-release job hunting. The program offers a weeklong job search workshop, one-on-one assistance with job placement, a resource room, and post-placement follow-up. Project RIO has more than 100 staff and 62 offices, and it serves some 16,000 individuals each year. The program has a pool of 12,000 employers who have hired parolees referred by Project RIO. In 1992, an independent evaluation found that 69 percent of RIO participants found jobs, compared with 36 percent of non-RIO parolees. Only 23 percent of high-risk RIO participants returned to prison, compared with 38 percent of comparable control groups.[184]

Chicago's **Safer Foundation** is a community-based provider of employment services for ex-offenders. Safer uses employment specialists to help place released prisoners in jobs and a small-group, peer-based approach in its basic educational skills program. These two programs help prepare individuals for life after incarceration. Special case managers are assigned to follow ex-offenders for one year after they have secured employment. In 2000, Safer placed 1,015 clients in jobs. Of these, nearly 60 percent were still employed after 30 days. Further, in a 1996 survey conducted by Safer, the majority of employers noted little or no difference between ex-prisoner job candidates referred by Safer and nonoffenders referred through more traditional channels. Also, in 2000, of the 168 16- to 21-year-old individuals Safer enrolled in the basic education course, nearly all (91 percent) completed the course and half (51 percent) received their general education degree (GED). A significant number of those who complete the course enter school, vocational training, or employment.[185]

Pioneer Human Services, based in Seattle, provides (among many other non-corrections-related services) housing, jobs, and social support for released prisoners, as well as sheltered workshops for hard-to-place offenders. What differentiates Pioneer Human Services from other work-release programs and social service agencies is that its funding comes almost entirely from the various businesses it operates.[186]

In-Prison Educational Programs

Beginning in the 1870s, American prisons began experimenting with programs aimed at improving the basic literacy and communication skills of prisoners. By the 1930s, prison rehabilitation efforts centered around educational programs, which had expanded greatly in size and scope. Today, most American prison systems offer a wide range of educational programs, from vocational training to postsecondary education courses. These diverse programs all aim to improve prisoners' behavior while in incarcerated, by facilitating the maturation and conscientiousness of the inmate, and to reduce recidivism, by improving employment prospects and by providing a broader frame of reference within which to make important decisions.[177]

Despite their longevity and prominence within the correctional system, rigorous evaluative research on the effectiveness of prison educational programs has been lacking. However, the available research does indicate that certain carefully designed and administered prison education programs can improve inmate behavior and reduce recidivism. For example, a recent study sponsored by the Virginia Department of Correctional Education tracked reincarceration rates among offenders in Virginia over a fifteen-year period and found that recidivism rates were 59 percent lower for those inmates who had participated in and completed prison educational programs versus those who had not participated.[178] Preliminary results from the largest and most comprehensive correctional education and recidivism study to date also show lower rates of recidivism among inmates who participated in these programs, although the findings are not as dramatic as the Virginia study. In this study of over 3,000 inmates, rates of reincarceration for offenders who participated in education programs were 20 percent lower than inmates who did not.[179] Moreover, certain studies that have attempted to measure the effect prison education programs have on post-release employment also show positive results. A 1994 meta-analysis indicated that in three of the four studies under investigation prison education programs significantly increased chances of securing employment following release from prison.[180]

Despite these promising findings, evidence suggests that funding for these programs has not kept pace with the recent expansion of the prison population. During the "get tough on crime" environment that dominated the 1990s, many states cut existing prison educational programs, often to fund new prisons. In California, for example, the number of prison teachers has dropped by 200 over the last 15 years, as the prison population grew from 30,000 to 160,000.[181] Also, in 1994 inmates were declared ineligible for college Pell grants, leaving many prisoners unable to pursue college degrees during their incarceration.

REENTRY AND HOUSING

An often overlooked challenge facing the returning prisoner is the issue of housing. One of the first things a prisoner must do upon release is find a place to stay. Housing presents problems, for several reasons. First, returning prisoners rarely have the financial resources or personal references necessary to compete for and secure housing in the private housing market. In addition, federal laws bar many ex-prisoners from public housing and federally assisted housing programs. And, some number of prisoners are not welcome back in their family home. For a combination of these and other reasons, some returning prisoners end up homeless, with all the attendant risks.

All returning prisoners must find a place to live when they leave prison. The initial barriers to finding affordable and stable housing are similar to those for finding employment. Most individuals leave prison without enough money for a security deposit on an apartment. Landlords typically require potential tenants to list employment and housing references and to disclose financial and criminal history information. For these reasons, offenders are often excluded from the private housing market. Importantly, public housing also may not be an option for returning prisoners. Federal housing policies permit—and in some cases require—public housing authorities, Section 8 providers, and other federally assisted housing programs to deny housing to individuals who have engaged in certain criminal activities.[187] The guidelines for denying housing are fairly broad and may encompass those who have, at any point in the past, engaged in drug-related activity, violent criminal activity, or other criminal activity that would negatively affect the health and safety of other residents. (Housing authorities have the right to obtain criminal records on tenants and applicants.)

Individuals who have been evicted from public housing because of drug-related criminal activity cannot reapply to live there for three years. However, housing providers do have discretion to shorten the three-year restriction for individuals who can show that they are getting help for their drug problem through participation in a treatment or rehabilitation program. Likewise, anyone who is found to be abusing alcohol or illegal drugs is ineligible for public housing benefits, although here too providers can make exceptions for individuals who are participating in treatment programs. Convicted sex offenders who are subject to a lifetime registration requirement, on the other hand, are ineligible for all public, Section 8, and other federally supported housing programs.

One option for ex-prisoners is to stay with family members following release. There is some evidence to suggest, however, that among the many who do,, these arrangements are often short-lived solutions. One reason is that family members living in public housing may not welcome a returning prisoner home when doing so may put their own housing situation at risk. These familial relationships may also be so severely strained and tenuous that staying with family members or friends is not a viable option.

Given the restrictions of the private housing market, the policies of public housing, and the host of other issues returning prisoners face, it is perhaps not surprising that many of them end up living on the streets. One study from the late 1980s estimated that as many as one quarter of all homeless individuals had served time in prison.[188] In California, the Department of Corrections reports that at any given time 10 percent of the state's parolees are homeless.[189] This rate is significantly higher in major urban areas such as San Francisco and Los Angeles, where as many as 30 to 50 percent of parolees are estimated to be homeless.[190]

Although homeless shelters may be a last resort for many former prisoners in need of housing, it is not always available. All federally funded shelters require that individuals be homeless for at least 24 hours before they are eligible for a bed. Also, shelters with limited bed space may be reluctant to house offenders. The period immediately following release, when a returning prisoner may be most tempted to fall back into old habits, is critical. Providing access to affordable housing options that will aid the transition back to the community may be an important factor in relapse prevention.

Loss of Civil Liberties

In addition to the substance abuse, health, housing, and employment issues facing returning prisoners, released inmates as a group experience a series of collateral consequences, most often as a result of a felony conviction. For example, in many states, convicted felons are precluded from voting, holding political office, serving on jury duty, owning a firearm, or holding certain jobs. In addition, they may temporarily or permanently lose eligibility for certain public benefit programs.[191]

Voting Rights. Denial of the right to vote has significant implications for individual offenders and, increasingly, for certain communities in the United States. Nearly all states restrict the voting rights of convicted felons in some way.[192] The laws of 46 states and the District of Columbia stipulate that convicted offenders cannot vote while in prison, and 32 states prohibit offenders on probation or parole from voting. In more than a dozen states, a convicted felon loses the right to vote for life.[193] According to one estimate, nearly 4 million Americans—one in fifty adults—are either currently or permanently prohibited from voting because of a felony conviction. Of these, 1.4 million are African American, accounting for 13 percent of the adult black male population. In states that impose lifetime voting bans on convicted felons, the aggregate consequences in African-American communities are profound. One in every four African-American men have lost the right to vote for life in Alabama, Florida, Iowa, Mississippi, New Mexico, Virginia, and Wyoming.[194] Viewed at the community level, these restrictions have far-reaching consequences for democratic participation and political influence.

Criminal Registration Requirements. Over the last 15 years the trend has been to extend the period of punishment beyond an individual's probation, prison, and parole sentence, particularly for sex offenders. In 1986, only eight states required released offenders to register with a police department in their area. A series of high-profile, violent crimes committed by released offenders resulted in legislative initiatives requiring offenders to register with law enforcement agencies upon their release. By 1998, convicted sex offenders in every state were subject to a registration requirement following release from prison. These registration requirements vary widely. While most states mandate sex offender registration for those convicted after the effective date of the legislation, several states made the requirement retroactive. Eight states require registration of all eligible offenders convicted before 1980. The durations of offender registration requirements range from 10 years to life; 12 states mandate lifetime registration of everyone in the registry. As of 1998, there were nearly 280,000 sex offenders listed in state sex offender registries across the country.[195]

CHAPTER 4

Implications of Prisoner Reentry for Families and Communities

One clear consequence of imprisonment is that relationships with families and the broader community are strained. Most prisoners are parents—about half of male inmates and two-thirds of female inmates leave at least one child behind when they enter the prison gates. In 1999, more than 1.5 million minor children had a parent who was incarcerated, an increase of more than a half-million since 1991. In some cases, the removal of a family member may be beneficial for those left behind—particularly someone who has been violent at home or draining needed financial resources to support a drug habit. But in many cases it is a traumatic event for families with consequences that reverberate well beyond an individual's release from prison. Further, for communities with high rates of removal and return of offenders, these consequences have far-reaching implications. This section outlines the consequences and implications of reentry from the perspective of the families and communities to which prisoners return.

THE IMPACT OF REENTRY ON FAMILIES AND CHILDREN OF FORMER PRISONERS

The growth in incarceration over the past two decades has significant implications for families and children of former prisoners. In 1999, more than half of all state inmates were parents of children below the age of 18—a total of more than 1.5 million children.[196] The substantial increase in the number of female offenders sentenced to prison in recent years—the female prisoner population has more than doubled since 1990[197]—contributes significantly to the number of inmates who have children. This is an important distinction, because incarcerated mothers and fathers typically have a different level of involvement with their children before incarceration, which affects the subsequent caregiving arrangement, ongoing contact during imprisonment, and reunification upon release.

Although removing particular individuals can clearly be beneficial for some families—resulting in more attention to children, more resources available, fewer distractions from home life, and less fear or actual violence in the home—there is considerable evidence that many children and families suffer when a parent is removed from the home. This section explores the consequences of the removal and release of offenders for child care, custody and parental rights, child welfare, and the future criminality of children.

Incarcerated males are fathers to 1.2 million children. Although only 44 percent of these fathers lived with their children prior to incarceration, most contributed income, child care, and social support.[198] Several studies have documented the desire of nonresident fathers to remain involved in their children's lives through regular visits and financial support.

At the same time, prison life disrupts these relationships between fathers and their children. Only 40 percent of incarcerated fathers report having weekly contact with their children, mostly by mail or phone.[199] And the frequency of contact decreases as the length of time served in prison increases.[200] Given that the majority of state prisoners (60 percent) are held in facilities more than 100 miles from their homes, it is not surprising that most fathers (57 percent) report never having a personal visit with their children after admission to prison.[201]

Although women represent a much smaller proportion of the prison population, the female prison population is growing faster than the male population. From the child's perspective, the incarceration of a mother has quite different consequences from incarceration of a father. First, because mothers are more likely to be the primary caregivers, a child's placement after a mother is incarcerated is more uncertain than when the father is imprisoned. Fewer than one-third of all children with an incarcerated mother remain with their fathers. Most are cared for by extended family—53 percent of children with an incarcerated mother live with a grandparent and 26 percent live with other relatives. Some children, however, become part of the foster care system. Ten percent of incarcerated mothers and 2 percent of incarcerated fathers report they have a child placed in foster care.[202]

Mothers also tend to stay in closer contact with their children while in prison. Nearly 80 percent reported monthly contact and 60 percent reported at least weekly contact. However, as with fathers, more than half of all mothers report never receiving a personal visit from their children. Visits are even more difficult for incarcerated mothers who, because of the scarcity of prisons for women, tend to be an average of 160 miles farther from their children than are incarcerated fathers.[203] Despite this separation, most mothers expect to be reunited with their children upon release.[204]

Incarceration of a parent is increasingly a factor in many children's lives. Two percent of all minor children in the United States and about 7 percent of all African-American children had a parent in state or federal prison in 1999.[205] How is the experience of having a parent incarcerated felt by these children and what are the long-term consequences? Unfortunately, such questions have received little empirical attention, and the studies that exist do little to parse

Of the soon-to-be-released prisoner population in 1997:[206]

- About two-thirds had children
- Nearly 60 percent had never married and another one quarter were divorced.

According to research conducted by Denise Johnston at the Center for Children of Incarcerated Parents, the family configurations of incarcerated parents and their children can be very complicated.[207] It is not uncommon for both incarcerated fathers and mothers to have children by more than one partner. This means that while 44 percent of fathers and 64 percent of mothers report living with their children prior to admission, they may have only lived with some of their children rather than all of their children.[208] Further, although a parent may have been living with their children before being sent to prison, that does not necessarily mean that the parent was the primary caregiver. These families may include extended family members who have taken on the role of primary caregiver. In Johnston's current study of female prisoners living in mother-child correctional facilities, less than one-third of the women had been living with all of their children prior to incarceration and even fewer were their children's primary caregiver.

One of every 14 African-American children has a parent in state or federal prison.[209]

out the causal connection between incarceration of parent and child outcomes.[210] What we do know is that children whose parents have been incarcerated experience a range of negative consequences, but we cannot say the extent to which these consequences are a direct result of a parent being incarcerated or the nature of family life in that household.[211] For instance, several studies have found that children of incarcerated parents are more likely to exhibit low self-esteem, depression, emotional withdrawal from friends and family, and inappropriate or disruptive behavior at home and in school. There is also some evidence to suggest that children of incarcerated parents are at high risk of future delinquency and/or criminal behavior.[212] Two studies have found that children of offenders are significantly more likely than other children to be arrested or incarcerated.[213]

Understanding the impact of parental incarceration on children is complicated because these consequences may be related to any number of conditions—the parent-child separation, the crime and arrest that preceded incarceration, or the general instability and inadequate care at home. Further, the degree to which a child is affected by incarceration of a parent rests on a number of variables, including the age at which the child is separated from the parent, the length of the separation, the level of disruption, the number and result of previous separation experiences, and the availability of family or community support.[214]

The role parents play in the development of their children's lives and the potential impact of a parent-child separation as a result of incarceration highlight the need to find ways to help families keep in touch during incarceration and reunite upon release. However, maintaining these relationships—between the parents and between the parent and child—during a period of incarceration can be difficult. Obstacles identified by the Women's Prison Association include inadequate information on visiting procedures, little help from correctional facilities about visiting arrangements, the time involved in traveling great distances to get to the correctional facility, visiting procedures that are uncomfortable or humiliating, and concerns about children's reactions to in-prison visits.[215] These circumstances can easily strain relationships between parents and their children.[216]

According to one expert, even struggling families can provide some level of "protective" support that may result in lower recidivism rates among released inmates. For example, one study found that, overall, prisoners with family ties during the period of incarceration do better when released than those without such ties.[217] And, as discussed in a sidebar earlier in this report, a small study by the Vera Institute of Justice reported that supportive families were an indicator of success across the board, correlating with lower drug use, greater likelihood of finding jobs, and reduced criminal activity.[218]

At the same time, there are situations where families are better off without a neglectful or abusive parent or partner in their lives. Some individuals may have been convicted of a crime of violence or abuse in the home, while others were convicted of different crimes but may exhibit a pattern of abuse. Likewise, some individuals are better served by not returning to a family environment

A Family-Focused Approach to Reentry: La Bodega de la Familia[219]

La Bodega de la Familia ("the family grocery"), on New York's Lower East Side, connects substance-abusing individuals and their families to services and supports in the community, including family case management, counseling and relapse prevention, and 24-hour crisis intervention. A project of the Vera Institute of Justice, La Bodega is built on the proposition that strengthening families will improve treatment outcomes, reduce the use of arrest and incarceration in response to relapse, and reduce the intrafamilial harms often associated with substance abuse. The program's primary service, family case management, engages the individual, family members, supervision officers, and treatment providers to develop a plan for tapping the family's strengths and supporting the individual's successful reintegration.

Many families are referred to the program by parole or probation. A La Bodega staff member accompanies parole officers on visits to prepare the family for a prisoner's release. Once the individual is released, the whole family is assessed to identify the strengths they bring to address the challenges of addiction, previous criminal history, and child welfare involvement. La Bodega case managers work with the family to develop a plan for services and set goals for the individuals and their family, broadly defined.

La Bodega also helps facilitate the relationship among families, former prisoners, and supervision officers. The New York State Division of Parole has assigned five parole officers to work exclusively with La Bodega families. During the initial community visit, family members are introduced to both the parole officer and La Bodega, and given the opportunity to have input on the reintegration process from the beginning. Throughout the period of supervision, individuals make regular visits with both their parole officers and La Bodega staff. And to the extent that the ex-prisoner's reintegration goals are related to supervision requirements, the parole officer is involved in all discussions on these issues and given regular progress reports. The program is now being evaluated by the Vera Institute of Justice, which will release its findings in 2001.[220]

still characterized by substance abuse, criminal behavior, and other negative influences that could act as triggers of past behaviors and habits.

Although children may be better off without a neglectful and abusive parent in their lives, there are many caring and committed incarcerated mothers and fathers who expect to resume their parenting role upon release. Recent legislative initiatives, however, have made it more difficult for incarcerated parents—particularly mothers—to reunite with their children upon release. For example, the 1997 Adoption and Safe Families Act, replacing the 1980 Adoption Assistance and Child Welfare Act, mandates termination of parental rights once a child has been in foster care for 15 or more of the past 22 months. Incarcerated women serve an average of 18 months in prison.[221] The result is that the average woman sentenced to prison whose children are placed in foster care could lose the right to reunite with her children upon release.

Welfare reform legislation could also make it very difficult for parents to rebuild a life with their children. As was discussed in an earlier section, returning prisoners are at a disadvantage for finding a job for various reasons. Access to public benefits that could help families find a stable footing following release has been limited under certain conditions. Individuals in violation of a condition of their parole or probation can be barred from receiving federal welfare benefits (TANF), food stamps, Supplemental Security Income, and access to public housing.[222] Further, individuals convicted of a drug felony are permanently banned from receiving TANF or food stamps. This could have profound implications for incarcerated mothers, because 35 percent are incarcerated for a drug charge.[223]

Incarceration and reentry have substantial impacts on a large and growing number of families—ranging from the loss of financial and emotional support to the social stigma attached to having a family member in prison. These complex relationships, combined with the great distance between many prisons and their home communities, require creative management on the part of the families, government agencies, and community support systems to minimize the harm to children and families.

THE IMPACT OF REENTRY ON COMMUNITIES

Returning prisoners are concentrated in a few states, a few core urban counties within those states, and a few neighborhoods within those counties. In 1998, for example, five states accounted for half of all releases, and 10 states accounted for 75 percent.[224] Within these states and others, prisoners typically return to a relatively few neighborhoods, which are already experiencing significant disadvantage. Some researchers have found that high concentrations of prisoner removal and return can further destabilize these communities, and that high incarceration rates can, under certain conditions, lead to even higher crime rates. A number of efforts are under way that leverage these concentrations—where community, corrections, service providers, and the private sector are creating partnerships to anticipate and address the population of prisoners returning home.

The majority of prisoners are released into counties that contain the central cities of metropolitan areas. In 1996, approximately two-thirds of state prisoners were released into these "core counties"—up from 50 percent in 1984.[225] This means that a higher percentage of a larger volume of prisoners are returning to a relatively small number of metropolitan areas. The central cities typically are poorer than neighboring areas, and they face other challenges, such as loss of labor market share to suburban regions.[226]

New research also suggests that large numbers of prisoners come from a relatively small number of neighborhoods within the central cities of the core counties. For example, in some Brooklyn neighborhoods, one out of eight parenting-age males is admitted to jail or prison in a single year.[227] Moreover, as figure 10 shows, the six police precincts with the highest number of residents on parole account for only 25 percent of the total population of Brooklyn, but the same six precincts are home to 55 percent of all the parolees in Brooklyn.[228] Looking at the block-group level (small areas within census tracts), one finds that 11 percent of the block groups account for 20 percent of the population in Brooklyn, yet are home to 50 percent of the parolees.

Figure 10. Parolees per Block Group, Brooklyn, N.Y.

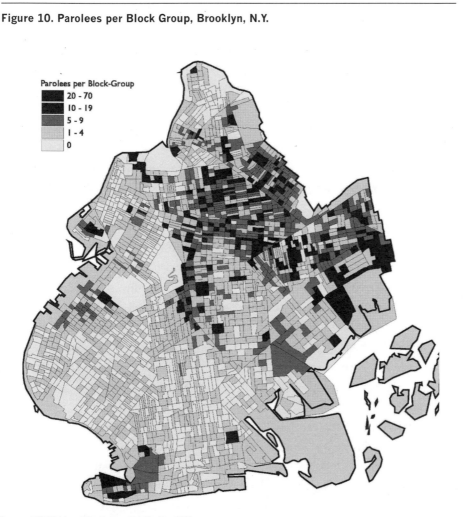

Parolees per Block-Group
- 20 - 70
- 10 - 19
- 5 - 9
- 1 - 4
- 0

Source: NYS Division of Parole Snapshot File, Nov. 2000.
Map produced by Charles Swartz & Eric Cadora. Community Justice Project, CASES. Copyright © 2001 CASES.

Community Concentrations

As can be seen in figure 10, returning prisoners may be concentrated in a relatively few neighborhoods. For example, in Brooklyn, 3 percent of the block groups account for 9 percent of the population, yet they house 26 percent of the parolees. Looked at differently, 11 percent of the block groups account for 20 percent of the population and 50 percent of all the parolees in Brooklyn.

Reentry Partnerships and Reentry Courts Initiatives

The Department of Justice has two initiatives under way to address prisoner reentry—the Reentry Partnerships and Reentry Courts Initiatives. The Reentry Partnerships Initiative involves institutional and community corrections, law enforcement, faith-based organizations, social services, victim support groups, and neighborhood organizations to build the monitoring, coordinating services, and community links that are essential to support the individual's successful reentry and to enhance public safety. Participating states are Florida, Maryland, Massachusetts, Missouri, Nevada, South Carolina, Vermont, and Washington.

The Reentry Courts concept draws on the authority of the court to promote positive behavior of returning prisoners—similar to the approach of drug courts but applied at the back end of a term of imprisonment. Graduated sanctions and incentives are integral to this model. Reentry Court sites are in California, Colorado, Delaware, Florida, Iowa, Kentucky, New York, Ohio, and West Virginia.

Congress has appropriated nearly $100 million in federal funds (FY 2001) to support a broad-based reentry initiative that spans three cabinet agencies—the Departments of Justice, Labor, and Health and Human Services. Under this initiative, state corrections and parole agencies, local workforce development agencies and treatment providers, community groups, and police organizations will be encouraged to devise collaborative reentry initiatives.

For more information on the Department of Justice pilot sites or the federal funding, see http://www.ojp.usdoj.gov/reentry/whats_new.htm.

Similarly, analysis conducted using data on Ohio state prisoners from Cuyahoga County (which includes the city of Cleveland) shows that two-thirds of the county's prisoners and most of the block groups with high rates of incarceration come from Cleveland. Concentrations are such that well under 1 percent of the block groups in the county account for approximately 20 percent of the county's prisoners. In such "high-rate" block groups, somewhere between 8 and 15 percent of the young black males are incarcerated on a given day.[230] Similar conclusions can be drawn from a study in Baltimore, where 15 percent of the neighborhoods accounted for 56 percent of prison releases.[231]

High rates of removal and return of offenders may further destabilize disadvantaged neighborhoods. Recent research by Todd Clear and Dina Rose indicates that high incarceration rates may disrupt a community's social network, affecting family formation, reducing informal control of children and income to families, and weakening ties among residents. The researchers posit that when removal and return rates hit a certain tipping point, they may actually result in *higher* crime rates, as the neighborhood becomes increasingly unstable and less coercive means of social control are undermined.[232]

Community concentrations are also significant because the economic, social, and emotional impact of reentry on individuals and families become compounded. These communities may have little capacity to address the needs of their residents, offenders and nonoffenders alike, such as substance abuse treatment, employment opportunities, health care, housing, and counseling. In California, for example, a study found significant gaps between the needs of parolees and available services: There are only 200 shelter beds for more than 10,000 homeless parolees, 4 mental health clinics for 18,000 psychiatric cases, and 750 treatment beds for 85,000 released substance abusers.[233] Physical proximity to services in the high-rate neighborhoods may be an issue as well. Clear and Rose looked at where ex-offenders (in Tallahassee, Fla.) lived, in relation to where the social services and supervision offices were located. They found that services and supervision offices were often very distant from the high-concentration neighborhoods that housed their clients and caseloads.

This mismatch between expenditures and community needs can be seen from a third perspective. Analysis by the Wisconsin Sentencing Commission found that approximately $2 million in criminal justice funds were spent in one year on arrest, prosecution, and incarceration of drug offenders in one Milwaukee neighborhood—the corner of a local park on 9th and Concordia streets—that suffered a high crime rate. Police had reportedly made 94 drug arrests at that particular corner within a three-month period. Despite the high conviction rate for these cases and the relatively severe sentences being handed out, the crime conditions at 9th and Concordia did not change. The Sentencing Commission asked the strategic question: Could those state resources have been invested differently to improve safety outcomes?[234]

This community-level analysis of the impact of removal and return has prompted new questions about effective ways to address reentry and reintegration. For example, would place-based strategies that involve a small team of parole officers working with local services be a more effective way to manage this population? Or could community-based social service providers, employers, neighborhood associations, faith institutions, and families work with the corrections and paroling authorities to prepare for prisoner returns, deter bad behavior, and enhance opportunities for reintegration?

New efforts are under way that center on community partnerships, problem-solving, and public safety. Building on the community policing model, this community supervision approach involves place-based supervision strategies and partnerships between law enforcement agencies and community residents. Such efforts may involve diverse entities—from prospective employers to social service agencies to family members to community corrections components to faith-based organizations. Each one has a unique role to play in anticipating and preparing for prisoner release. A number of small-scale reentry experiments are under way to test some of these coordinated, proactive strategies. The goal of these pilot efforts is to improve risk management of released prisoners by strengthening individual and community support systems, enhancing surveillance and monitoring, and repairing the harm done to victims. (See "Reentry Partnerships and Reentry Courts Initiatives" sidebar.)

A community-based perspective on prisoner reentry raises important questions about the role of the public in the justice system. In the mid-1990s, the Vermont Department of Corrections commissioned market research to find out what the public expects from the criminal justice system and from offenders.[235] They found that citizens want safety from violent offenders, accountability for the offense, treatment for the individual, and involvement in decision-making. They want offenders to accept responsibility for their behavior, to acknowledge their wrongdoing (perhaps even with an apology), and to repair the harm done to victims and the community. Citizens signaled a willingness to be involved in justice strategies, feeling they could contribute valuably in helping corrections create a safe and just community. This approach to the justice process, sometimes called "community justice," opens up new possibilities for the individual, the system, and the community.

What Can Communities Do about Reentry?

- Begin working with prisoners and the department of corrections before prisoners are released to arrange for jobs, housing, treatment, and health care upon release.

- Meet prisoners upon release, helping navigate the first hours or days in the community.

- Create or build on neighborhood-based networks of workforce development partners and local businesses who will target the preparation and employment of parolees.

- Engage local community-based organizations that can learn how to help family members support the parolee to overcome substance abuse problems, stay employed, and meet the overall requirements of his or her supervision and reintegration plan.

- Involve local faith institutions that can facilitate mentoring support in the neighborhood to parolees and their family members.

- Provide parolees opportunities to participate in community service and demonstrate that they can be community assets rather than simply neighborhood liabilities.

- Develop coalitions of resident leaders who will oversee the reentry efforts and provide accountability for community and offender obligations.

CHAPTER 5

Conclusion

This monograph on the dimensions and consequences of prisoner reentry has sought to accomplish two different goals: first, to shed light on some old issues that lie at the core of our philosophy of criminal justice and second, to highlight new opportunities for improving the outcomes of the process of prisoner reintegration.

The phenomenon of prisoner reentry is not new, of course, nor are the questions it raises. Ever since prisons were built, society has been confronted with the implications of that moment when a prison sentence is completed and the prisoner returns home. What are the mutual obligations of the ex-offender, his or her family, the victim, the community, and the state? What are the terms on which reintegration can be achieved? What social goals are to be pursued following the prisoner's return home, and who is responsible for them? How is failure defined, and how does society respond to the inevitable failures?

Generations of philosophers, legal scholars, practitioners, and members of the general public have wrestled with these fundamental questions. The contemporary portrait of prisoner reentry contained in these pages leads to the conclusion that the goal of prisoner reintegration has not yet received sufficient attention. One cannot escape the conclusion that the attention focused on prison expansion and the frenetic pace of sentencing reform over the past generation have been at the expense of systematic thinking about the goals and processes of prisoner reentry. The reductions in per capita funding for parole supervision, at a time of substantial increases in funding for prison construction, present a clear example of the policy tradeoff. Increasing the size of the prison population, as we have seen, does not reduce the problems associated with prisoner reentry—those problems are compounded and redefined as more people leave prison.

Similarly, the movement from indeterminate sentencing to determinate sentencing—and the related shift from discretionary prison terms to mandatory prison terms—has far-reaching consequences for the process of reintegration. Even if prison populations had not expanded, this shift in sentencing philosophy alone would require a fresh look at our expectations for prisoner reentry. If release from prison is automatic, does that change the incentives of the prisoner and the obligations of the correctional agency to prepare for the prisoner's release? If the prisoner walks out the prison door having completed his sentence, is there no societal interest in his reintegration?

The dimensions of prisoner reentry described here argue for a reexamination of the nexus among the jurisprudence of sentencing, the mission of corrections agencies, the availability and quality of services for prisoners and their families, and the social goal of prisoner reintegration.

At the same time, a focus on reentry illuminates new ways to approach these questions, some of them quite simple, some more complex. For example, a focus on the moment of release, with its attendant risks and opportunities, suggests that correctional agencies and community groups could create new links to smooth the transition from prison to liberty. Something as simple as ensuring that the prisoner has proper identification, a roof over his or her head, and a community agency to report to the next day may avert some failures of the immediate transitional phase. Even more substantial linkages come to mind when the health and substance abuse needs of returning prisoners are being considered—such as links to health care providers, drug treatment, transitional work environments, family counseling, and faith institutions. This strategy suggests moving the reentry planning process into the prison itself so that these linkages are created well before the moment of release.

While prisoner reentry is ultimately felt at the community level, state agencies play a large role in the management of the reentry process. Using the "levers" of conditional supervision and the tools of graduated sanctions, criminal justice agencies could play an enhanced role in deterring criminal behavior and reducing drug use.[236] But government neither could nor should manage reentry alone. There are various opportunities for supervision agencies to work in concert with treatment providers, law enforcement, and the community to employ problem-solving methodologies that address the situational risks of reoffending, such as high-risk places, drug relapse, and reunification with criminal peers. These innovations do not require a shift in jurisprudence so much as the articulation of a new goal—shared among state corrections and parole agencies, and local organizations—to improve the likelihood of a successful return to the community.

Finally, prisoner reentry raises important questions about the ultimate objectives of the reentry process. Public safety remains an essential yardstick. This monograph has identified the safety risks posed by returning prisoners as well as a number of interventions that have been proven successful at reducing those risks. Renewed attention to prisoner reentry, if carefully implemented, has the potential to improve the safety of the communities and families most affected by the return of prisoners. Yet this portrait of reentry's impact underscores the wide variety of related objectives. Could improvements in prisoner reentry produce gains in public health? Reductions in levels of drug use in a community? Improved worker productivity? Measurable enhancements in child development and father-child relationships? Would a focus on prisoner reentry create a new sense of civic attachment on the part of both the returning prisoners and those involved in their transition to communal life?

This broader view of prisoner reentry suggests that the ultimate goal is perhaps best conceptualized as social reintegration, not just as reductions in recidivism. This view also envisions a new partnership of public and private entities that have an interest in improving those outcomes, not only out of concern for the former prisoners, but out of concern for those whose well-being is affected by the dynamics of their transition from prison to community. This broader focus, in turn, should lend new richness to the contemporary debates over those age-old questions of the purposes of the criminal law and the goals of sentencing.

References

1. The Bureau of Justice Statistics estimates that 585,400 prisoners were released in 2000. A.J. Beck, "State and Federal Prisoners Returning to the Community: Findings from the Bureau of Justice Statistics." Paper presented at the First Reentry Courts Initiative Cluster Meeting, Washington, D.C., April 13, 2000. For more information, see http://www.ojp.usdoj.gov/bjs/pub/pdf/sfprc.pdf.

2. Bureau of Justice Statistics, U.S. Department of Justice, "Direct expenditure on criminal justice, by level of government, 1982-97." http://www.ojp.usdoj.gov/bjs/glance/expgov.txt. (Accessed March 20, 2001.)

3. A.J. Beck, "Prisoners in 1999." *Bureau of Justice Statistics, Bulletin*. Washington, D.C.: U.S. Department of Justice, Bureau of Justice Statistics, NCJ 183476, August 2000.

4. A. Blumstein and A.J. Beck, "Population Growth in U.S. Prisons, 1980-1996." In M. Tonry and J. Petersilia (Eds.), *Prisons*. Chicago: University of Chicago Press, 1999.

5. Of note, aside from drug offenses, the adult arrest rate per crime remained remarkably stable from 1980 to 1996. The increasing prison population results from a rise in the use of incarceration in the sanctioning phase, coupled with a significant growth in the time served by prisoners. According to Blumstein and Beck, "Time served is the single factor influencing prison population that has been increasing steadily during the 1990s." See Blumstein and Beck, 1999, "Population Growth in U.S. Prisons, 1980-1996," p. 56.

6. See Beck, 2000, "Prisoners in 1999."

7. J. Travis, "But They All Come Back: Rethinking Prisoner Reentry." *Sentencing & Corrections, Issues for the 21st Century*, 7: Washington, D.C.: National Institute of Justice, NCJ 181413, 2000.

8. The 1977 figure comes from Bureau of Justice Statistics, U.S. Department of Justice, "Sentenced Prisoners Released from State or Federal Jurisdiction." http://www.ojp.usdoj.gov/bjs/dtdata.htm#justice. (Posted June 9, 2000. Accessed February 28, 2001.)

   The 2000 estimate comes from Beck, 2000, "State and Federal Prisoners Returning to the Community: Findings from the Bureau of Justice Statistics."

9. See Beck, 2000, "Prisoners in 1999."

10. M. Tonry, "The Fragmentation of Sentencing and Corrections in America." *Sentencing & Corrections, Issues for the 21st Century*, 1. Washington, D.C.: National Institute of Justice, NCJ 175721, September 1999.

11. M. Tonry, *Sentencing Matters*. New York, New York: Oxford University Press, 1996.

12. As of 1998, 17 states had created sentencing commissions, quasi-independent administrative bodies that have designed sentencing grids that significantly constrain judicial sentencing discretion. See D.B. Rottman, C.R. Flango, M.T. Cantrell, R. Hansen, and N. LaFountain, "State Court Organization 1998." Washington, D.C.: U.S. Department of Justice, Bureau of Justice Statistics, NCJ 178932, 2000. Legislation creating mandatory minimum sentences has been enacted in all 50 states. See J. Austin, C. Jones, J. Kramer, and P. Renninger, "National Assessment of Structured Sentencing, Final Report." Washington, D.C.: U.S. Department of Justice, Bureau of Justice Assistance, NCJ 167557, 1995. Three-strikes laws have lengthened prison terms for persistent offenders in 24 states. See J. Austin, J. Clark, P. Hardyman, and D.A. Henry, "Impact of 'Three Strikes and You're Out.'" *Punishment & Society*, 1, 131-162, 1999. Forty states have enacted truth-in-sentencing laws requiring that violent offenders serve at least 50 percent of their sentences in prison; of these 40 states, 27 and the District of Columbia require violent offenders to serve at least 85 percent of their sentences in prison. See P.M. Ditton and D.J. Wilson, "Truth in Sentencing in State Prisons." Bureau of Justice Statistics, Special Report. Washington, D.C.: U.S. Department of Justice, Bureau of Justice Statistics, NCJ 170032, January 1999.

13. M. Lynch, "Waste Managers? New Penology, Crime Fighting, and the Parole Agent Identity." *Law and Society Review*, 32, 839-869, 1998.

14. J.P. Lynch and W.J. Sabol. Forthcoming. "Prisoner Reentry in Perspective." Urban Institute *Crime Policy Report*. Washington, D.C.: Urban Institute.

15. J. Petersilia, "Parole and Prisoner Reentry in the United States." In M. Tonry and J. Petersilia (Eds.), *Prisons*. Chicago: University of Chicago Press, 1999.

[16] M. Kleiman, "Getting Deterrence Right: Applying Tipping Models and Behavioral Economics to the Problems of Crime Control." *Perspectives on Crime and Justice: 1998-1999 Lecture Series, 3.* Washington, D.C.: National Institute of Justice, NCJ 178244, 1999.

[17] See Blumstein and Beck, 1999, "Population Growth in U.S. Prisons, 1980-1996."

[18] At the same time, because length of stay for parole violators is, on average, significantly less than a sentence for a new commitment, parole violators do not account for a large share of the growth in the prison population. See Blumstein and Beck, 1999, "Population Growth in U.S. Prisons, 1980-1996."

[19] A.J. Beck and B.E. Shipley, "Recidivism of Prisoners Released in 1983." Bureau of Justice Statistics, Special Report. Washington, D.C.: U.S. Department of Justice, Bureau of Justice Statistics, NCJ 116261, April 1989.

[20] Note that each arrest could involve up to six charges, so there were fewer than 326,746 *incidents* for which the releasees were arrested.

[21] A small fraction of offenders are responsible for a disproportionate share of crime. For example, 5 percent of the 1983 release cohort in the Bureau of Justice Statistics study accounted for 19 percent of the 1,700,000 arrests this group was charged with (either prior to their imprisonment or following release). See Beck and Shipley, 1989, "Recidivism of Prisoners Released in 1983." Generally, characteristics of "high-rate" offenders include a criminal record for violent and drug offenses, very frequent use of multiple types of illegal drugs, early involvement in criminal activity, and use of serious illegal drugs as a juvenile. They are also typically "occupationally unstable," younger than other offenders, and often have a history of violence as a juvenile. See J.R. Chaiken and M.R. Chaiken, "Varieties of Criminal Behavior." Washington, D.C.: U.S. Department of Justice, National Institute of Justice, R 2814 NIJ, 1982. For a discussion on the relationship of certain risk factors and rearrest rates for the 1983 cohort, see Beck and Shipley, 1989, "Recidivism of Prisoners Released in 1983."

[22] M. Rennison, "Criminal Victimization 1999: Changes 1998-1999 with Trends 1993-1999." *Bureau of Justice Statistics, National Crime Victimization Survey.* Washington, D.C.: U.S. Department of Justice, Bureau of Justice Statistics, NCJ 182734, August 2000.

[23] D.J. Levin, P.A. Langan, and J.M. Brown, "State Court Sentencing of Convicted Felons, 1996." Washington, D.C.: U.S. Department of Justice, Bureau of Justice Statistics, NCJ 175708, February 2000.

[24] D.M. Kennedy, "Pulling Levers: Chronic Offenders, High-Crime Settings, and a Theory of Prevention." *Valparaiso University Law Review,* 31, 2, 449-484, Spring 1997. Of course, where an individual lives and where he or she commits the crime are often different places. Nonetheless, the Boston experience and others illustrate the nexus between neighborhoods, criminal activity, and supervision strategies.

[25] W. Spelman, "The Limited Importance of Prison Expansion." In A. Blumstein and J. Wallman (Eds.), *The Crime Drop in America.* Cambridge, United Kingdom: Cambridge University Press, 2000; and R. Rosenfeld, "Patterns in Adult Homicide: 1980-1995." In A. Blumstein and J. Wallman (Eds.), *The Crime Drop in America.* Cambridge, United Kingdom: Cambridge University Press, 2000.

[26] See W. Spelman's discussion in "The Crime Decline: Why and What's Next." Forthcoming. Washington, D.C.: Urban Institute.

[27] T.R. Clear, D.R. Rose, and J.A. Ryder, "Coercive Mobility and the Community: The Impact of Removing and Returning Offenders." Paper prepared for the Reentry Roundtable, Washington, D.C., October 12 and 13, 2000.

[28] T.J. Ambrosio and V. Schiraldi, "From Classrooms to Cell Blocks: A National Perspective." Washington, D.C.: Justice Policy Institute, 1997.

[29] See Beck, 2000, "State and Federal Prisoners Returning to the Community: Findings from the Bureau of Justice Statistics."

[30] For a more detailed discussion on the characteristics of returning prisoners, see forthcoming Lynch and Sabol, "Prisoner Reentry in Perspective."

[31] Violent offenses include murder, negligent and nonnegligent manslaughter, rape, sexual assault, robbery, assault, extortion, intimidation, criminal endangerment, and other violent offenses. Drug offenses include possession, manufacturing, trafficking, and other drug offenses.

[32] T.P. Bonczar and L.E. Glaze, "Probation and Parole in the United States, 1998." *Bureau of Justice Statistics, Bulletin.* Washington, D.C.: U.S. Department of Justice, Bureau of Justice Statistics, NCJ 160092, August 1999.

[33] Thirteen percent of parolees have an education level below eighth grade, and 45 percent have an educational level between ninth and eleventh grades. Bureau of Justice Statistics, U.S. Department of Justice, *National Corrections Reporting Program.* Washington, D.C.: U.S. Department of Justice, Bureau of Justice Statistics, 1997.

[34] See Bonczar and Glaze, 1999, "Probation and Parole in the United States, 1998."

[35] The fact that the share of prisoners convicted of violent offenses has increased faster than the proportion of reentry cohorts consisting of violent offenders indicates that future reentry cohorts are likely to include more violent offenders. See Lynch and Sabol, forthcoming, "Prisoner Reentry in Perspective."

[36] See forthcoming Lynch and Sabol, "Prisoner Reentry in Perspective." (Analysis based on Bureau of Justice Statistics NPS-1 data.)

[37] Bureau of Justice Statistics, U.S. Department of Justice, *Correctional Populations in the United States, 1997.* Washington, D.C.: U.S. Department of Justice, Bureau of Justice Statistics, NCJ 177613, November 2000.

[38] See Beck, 2000, "Prisoners in 1999."

[39] See forthcoming Lynch and Sabol, "Prisoner Reentry in Perspective."

[40] See Beck, 2000, "State and Federal Prisoners Returning to the Community: Findings from the Bureau of Justice Statistics."

[41] T.M. Hammett, "Health-Related Issues in Prisoner Reentry to the Community." Paper prepared for the Reentry Roundtable, Washington, D.C., October 12 and 13, 2000.

[42] California Department of Corrections, *Preventing Parolee Failure Program: An Evaluation.* Sacramento: California Department of Corrections, 1997.

[43] See Hammett, 2000, "Health-Related Issues in Prisoner Reentry to the Community."

[44] T.P. Bonczar, and A.J. Beck, "Lifetime Likelihood of Going to State or Federal Prison." Bureau of Justice Statistics, Special Report. Washington, D.C.: U.S. Department of Justice, Bureau of Justice Statistics, NCJ 160092, March 1997.

[45] *Ibid.*

[46] See Beck, 2000, "Prisoners in 1999."

47 B. Western and R. Pettit, "Incarceration and Racial Inequality in Men's Employment." *Industrial and Labor Relations Review*, 54, 3-16, 2000.

48 S. Klein, J. Petersilia, and S. Turner, "Race and Imprisonment Decisions in California." *Science*, 247, 812-816, Feb. 16, 1990.

49 C. Mumola and A. Beck, "Prisoners in 1996." Washington, D.C.: U.S. Department of Justice, Bureau of Justice Statistics, 1997.

50 *Ibid.*

51 Bureau of Justice Statistics, U.S. Department of Justice, *Correctional Populations in the United States, 1996*. Washington, D.C.: U.S. Department of Justice, Bureau of Justice Statistics, NCJ 170013, April 1999.

52 D. Johnston and K. Gabel, "Incarcerated Parents." In K. Gabel and D. Johnston (Eds.), *Children of Incarcerated Parents*. New York: Lexington Books, 1995.

53 D.T. Courtwright, "The Drug War's Hidden Toll." *Issues in Science and Technology*, 13.2, 73, Winter 1996.

    See also W.A. Darity Jr. and S. Myers Jr., 1995, "Family Structure and the Marginalization of Black Men: Policy Implications." In M.B. Tucker and C. Mitchel-Kernan (Eds.), *The Decline in Marriage Among African-Americans: Causes, Consequences, and Policy Implications*. New York: Russell Sage Foundation, 1995.

54 M. Dallao, "Coping with Incarceration from the Other Side of the Bars." *Corrections Today*, 59, 96-98, 1997.

55 L.A. Greenfeld and T.L. Snell, "Women Offenders." Bureau of Justice Statistics, Special Report. Washington, D.C.: U.S. Department of Justice, Bureau of Justice Statistics, NCJ 175688, December 1999.

56 *Ibid.*

57 *Ibid.*

58 B.E. Richie, "Issues Incarcerated Women Face When They Return to Their Communities." Paper prepared for the Reentry Roundtable, Washington, D.C., October 12 and 13, 2000.

59 *Ibid.*

60 U.S. Bureau of the Census. 1998. "Unpublished Tables—Marital Status and Living Arrangements: March 1998 (Update)." http://www.census.gov/population/www/socdemo/ms-la.html. (Accessed on April 12, 2001.)

61 See Richie, 2000, "Issues Incarcerated Women Face When They Return to Their Communities."

62 *Ibid.*

63 *Ibid.*

64 J. Hagan and J. Petty, "Returning Captives of the American War on Drugs: Issues of Community and Family Reentry." Paper prepared for the Reentry Roundtable, Washington, D.C., October 12 and 13, 2000.

65 See Petersilia, 1999, "Parole and Prisoner Reentry in the United States."

66 See Ditton and Wilson, 1999, "Truth in Sentencing in State Prisons."

67 Bureau of Justice Statistics, U.S. Department of Justice, "Prisoners Released Unconditionally from State or Federal Jurisdiction, 1977-98." http://www.ojp.usdoj.gov/bjs/dtdata.htm#time. (Accessed March 20, 2001.)

68 See Bureau of Justice Statistics, U.S. Department of Justice, 2000, *Correctional Populations in the United States, 1997*. Also see Ditton and Wilson, 1999, "Truth in Sentencing in State Prisons."

69 J.C. Runda, E.E. Rhine, and R.E. Wetter, *The Practice of Parole Boards*. Lexington, KY: Association of Paroling Authorities, International, 1994.

70 Nearly one-third of the unconditional releases from state prison (as proxied by first releases in the National Corrections Reporting Program states) were individuals who had been sentenced for a violent offense. *National Corrections Reporting Program*, Unpublished table, Washington, D.C.: Bureau of Justice Statistics, 1998.

71 There are exceptions, of course. In Ohio, for example, some lower-risk prisoners are released at the end of their term because it was determined at the time of sentencing that they did not require post-prison supervision. Additionally, some prisoners waive their right to early release under community supervision in favor of serving out their full term and are thereby free of any criminal justice supervision once released.

72 G.G. Gaes, T.J. Flanagan, L.L Motuik, and L. Stewart, "Adult Correctional Treatment." In M. Tonry and J. Petersilia (Eds.), *Prisons*. Chicago: University of Chicago Press, 1999.

73 *Ibid.*

74 C. Riveland, "Prison Management Trends, 1975-2025." In M. Tonry and J. Petersilia (Eds.), *Prisons*. Chicago: University of Chicago Press, 1999.

75 See forthcoming Lynch and Sabol, "Prisoner Reentry in Perspective."

76 See Beck, 2000, "State and Federal Prisoners Returning to the Community: Findings from the Bureau of Justice Statistics."

77 J. Austin, M.A. Bruce, L. Carroll, P.L. McCall, and S.C. Richards, "The Use of Incarceration in the United States." Paper prepared for the annual meeting of the American Society of Criminology, San Francisco, November 2000.

78 See forthcoming Lynch and Sabol, "Prisoner Reentry in Perspective."

79 I. Waller, *Men Released From Prison*. Toronto: University of Toronto Press, 1974.

80 K. Adams, "Adjusting to Prison Life." In *Crime and Justice: A Review of Research, Volume 16*. Chicago: University of Chicago Press, 1992.

81 J. J. Stephan, "State Prison Expenditures, 1996." Washington, D.C.: U.S. Department of Justice, Bureau of Justice Statistics, NCJ 172211, August 1999.

82 See Austin et al., 2000, "The Use of Incarceration in the United States."

83 E. Zamble and F.J. Porporino, *Coping, Behavior, and Adaptation in Prison Inmates*. New York: Springer, 1988; E. Zamble and V.L. Quinsey, *The Criminal Recidivism Process*. Cambridge, U.K.: Cambridge University Press, 1997.

84 Research Council of the American Correctional Association, "A Survey of Correctional Agencies' Research Topics and Interests." *Corrections Compendium*, 25, 8, 2-25, August 2000.

85 M. Nelson, P. Deess, and C. Allen, *The First Month Out: Post-Incarceration Experiences in New York City*. New York: Vera Institute of Justice, September 1999.

86 See American Correctional Association, 2000, "A Survey of Correctional Agencies' Research Topics and Interests."

[87] S. Turner and J. Petersilia, "Work Release: Recidivism and Corrections Costs in Washington State." *NIJ Research In Brief.* Washington, D.C.: National Institute of Justice, December 1996.

[88] See Nelson, Deess, and Allen, 1999, *The First Month Out: Post-Incarceration Experiences in New York City.*

[89] See Beck, 2000, "State and Federal Prisoners Returning to the Community: Findings from the Bureau of Justice Statistics."

[90] Bureau of Justice Statistics, U.S. Department of Justice, *National Corrections Reporting Program.* Washington, D.C.: U.S. Department of Justice, Bureau of Justice Statistics, various years.

[91] In many jurisdictions the parole supervision function is called something else (community supervision, supervised released, etc.), but it is functionally parole.

[92] 713,000 is a 1999 figure. See Bureau of Justice Statistics, U.S. Department of Justice, "Correctional Populations in the United States, 1980-1999." http://www.ojp.usdoj.gov/bjs/glance/corr2.txt. (Accessed February 28, 2001.)

[93] J. Petersilia, "Prisoners Returning to Communities: Political, Economic, and Social Consequences." Paper prepared for the Reentry Roundtable, Washington, D.C., October 12 and 13, 2000.

[94] See forthcoming Lynch and Sabol, "Prisoner Reentry in Perspective."

[95] See Petersilia, 2000, "Prisoners Returning to Communities: Political, Economic, and Social Consequences."

[96] See Bonczar and Glaze, 1999, "Probation and Parole in the United States, 1998."

[97] See Petersilia, 1999, "Parole and Prisoner Reentry in the United States."

[98] J. Petersilia, "A Decade of Experimenting with Intermediate Sanctions: What Have We Learned?" In *Perspectives on Crime and Justice.* Washington, D.C.: National Institute of Justice, 1998.

[99] J. Petersilia and S. Turner, "Intensive Probation and Parole." In M. Tonry (Ed.), *Crime and Justice: A Review of Research, Vol. 17.* Chicago: University of Chicago Press, 1993.

[100] L. Sherman, D. Gottfredson, D. MacKenzie, J. Eck, P. Reuter, and S. Bushway, *Preventing Crime: What Works, What Doesn't, What's Promising.* College Park: University of Maryland, 1997.

[101] Reinventing Probation Council, *Transforming Probation Through Leadership: The "Broken Windows" Model.* Center for Civic Innovation and the Robert A. Fox Leadership Program.

[102] Another 9 percent of adults leaving parole did not successfully complete parole because they had absconded. See Bonczar and Glaze, 1999, "Probation and Parole in the United States, 1998." The 206,000 figure is from Bureau of Justice Statistics, 2000, "Conditional Release Violators Returned to State or Federal Jurisdiction." Washington, D.C.: U.S. Department of Justice, Bureau of Justice Statistics, National Prisoner Statistics Data Series (NPS 1), August 2000. http://www.ojp.usdoj.gov/bjs/dtdata.htm#justice. (Accessed February 2001.)

[103] See Beck, 2000, "Prisoners in 1999." Also see A.J. Beck, 1999, "Understanding Growth in U.S. Prison and Parole Populations." Paper presented at the Annual Conference on Criminal Justice Research and Evaluation: Enhancing Policy and Practice, Washington, D.C., July 1999.

[104] Of the 42 percent returned to prison, 13 percent were for a new sentence, 29 percent for a technical violation. See Bonczar and Glaze, 1999, "Probation and Parole in the United States, 1998."

[105] R.L. Cohen, "Probation and Parole Violators in State Prison, 1991." Washington, D.C.: U.S. Department of Justice, Bureau of Justice Statistics, NCJ 149076, August 1995.

[106] See Petersilia, 1999, "Parole and Prisoner Reentry in the United States."

[107] P. B. Burke, "Policy-Driven Responses to Probation and Parole Violations." Washington, D.C., U.S. Department of Justice, National Institute of Corrections, March 1997.

[108] National Institute of Corrections, "Status Report on Parole, 1995: Results of an NIC Survey." Washington, D.C., U.S. Department of Justice, National Institute of Corrections, November 1995.

[109] Bureau of Justice Statistics, "Sentenced Prisoners Admitted to State or Federal Jurisdiction." Washington D.C.: U.S. Department of Justice, Bureau of Justice Statistics, National Prisoner Statistics Data Series (NPS 1), August 2000. http://www.ojp.usdoj.gov/bjs/dtdata.htm#justice. (Accessed February 2001.)

[110] C.J. Mumola, "Substance Abuse and Treatment, State and Federal Prisoners, 1997." Bureau of Justice Statistics, Special Report. Washington, D.C.: U.S. Department of Justice, Bureau of Justice Statistics, NCJ 172871, January 1999.

[111] See Beck, 2000, "State and Federal Prisoners Returning to the Community: Findings from the Bureau of Justice Statistics."

[112] See Mumola, 1999, "Substance Abuse and Treatment, State and Federal Prisoners, 1997."

[113] H.K. Wexler, D.S. Lipton, and B.D. Johnson, "A Criminal Justice System Strategy for Treating Cocaine-Heroin Abusing Offenders in Custody." Washington, D.C.: National Institute of Justice, NCJ 113915, 1998.

[114] See Gaes et al., 1999, "Adult Correctional Treatment." See also Harrison, 2000, "The Challenge of Reintegrating Drug Offenders in the Community."

[115] The most widely adopted (and evaluated) program is the Cognitive Thinking Skills Program (CTSP) developed by Robert Ross and Elizabeth Fabiano. It has been widely implemented in several correctional systems, including the United States, Canada, Europe, New Zealand, and throughout the British prison system. See Gaes et al., 1999, "Adult Correctional Treatment," p. 374.

[116] See Gaes et al., 1999, "Adult Correctional Treatment."

[117] *Ibid.*

[118] B.M.M. Pelissier et al., "TRIAD Drug Treatment Evaluation Project Six-Month Interim Report." Federal Bureau of Prisons, Office of Research and Evaluation, January 31, 1998.

[119] See Gaes et al., 1999, "Adult Correctional Treatment."

[120] See Harrison, 2000, "The Challenge of Reintegrating Drug Offenders in the Community." See also Gaes et al., 1999, "Adult Correctional Treatment."

121 See Gaes et al., 1999, "Adult Correctional Treatment."

122 See Harrison. "The Challenge of Reintegrating Drug Offenders in the Community." Paper presented at the Reentry Roundtable, Washington, D.C., October 12-13, 2000. See also Gaes et al., 1999, "Adult Correctional Treatment."

123 Formal treatment includes professional counseling, detoxification units, residential facilities, and maintenance drug programs. When one includes participation in other drug abuse programs, such as self-help groups and educational programs, the participation rates increase to 24 percent of the 1997 prison population, down from 30 percent in 1991. See Bureau of Justice Statistics, U.S. Department of Justice, 2000, *Correctional Populations in the United States, 1997.*

124 See Beck, 2000, "State and Federal Prisoners Returning to the Community: Findings from the Bureau of Justice Statistics."

125 See Bureau of Justice Statistics, U.S. Department of Justice, 2000, *Correctional Populations in the United States, 1997.*

126 See Beck, 2000, "State and Federal Prisoners Returning to the Community: Findings from the Bureau of Justice Statistics."

127 See Gaes et al., 1999, "Adult Correctional Treatment."

128 A.I. Leshner, "Addiction Is a Brain Disease—and It Matters." *National Institute of Justice Journal*, 237, 2-6, 1998.

129 T.M. Hammett, "Health-Related Issues in Prisoner Reentry to the Community." Paper prepared for the Reentry Roundtable, Washington, D.C., October 12 and 13, 2000.

130 National Center on Addiction and Substance Abuse (CASA) at Columbia University. *Behind Bars: Substance Abuse and America's Prison Population.* New York: CASA, January 1998.

131 L. M. Maruschak and A.J. Beck, "Medical Problems of Inmates, 1997." Bureau of Justice Statistics, Special Report. Washington, D.C.: U.S. Department of Justice, Bureau of Justice Statistics, NCJ 181644, January 2001.

132 J.P. Caulkins, C.P. Rydell, W. Schwabe, and J.R. Chiesa, "Mandatory Minimum Sentences: Throwing Away the Key or the Taxpayers' Money?" RAND publication MR-827-DPRC, 1997.

133 D.R. Gerstein, R.A. Johnson, H.J. Harwood, D. Fountain, N. Suter, and K. Malloy, *Evaluating Recovery Services: The California Drug and Alcohol Treatment Assessment (CALDATA).* Sacramento, CA: California Department of Alcohol and Drug Programs, 1994.

134 Research Council of the American Correctional Association, Corrections Compendium, "Correctional Budgets." *Corrections Compendium,* 25, 12, 8-17, December 2000.

135 A.J. Lurigio (forthcoming), "Effective Services for Parolees with Mental Illnesses." *Crime and Delinquency.*

136 P.M. Ditton, "Mental Health and Treatment of Inmates and Probationers." Bureau of Justice Statistics, Special Report. Washington, D.C.: U.S. Department of Justice, Bureau of Justice Statistics, NCJ 174463, July 1999.

137 L.M. Maruschak, "HIV in Prisons 1997." Bureau of Justice Statistics, Bulletin. Washington, D.C.: U.S. Department of Justice, Bureau of Justice Statistics, NCJ 178284, November 1999.

138 See Hammett, 2000, "Health-Related Issues in Prisoner Reentry to the Community."

139 *Ibid.*

140 Medical problems were more prevalent among inmates who had been homeless or unemployed prior to incarceration. Of the state inmates who reported that they had been homeless for some period of time in the year before incarceration, nearly half reported a physical impairment or mental condition and one-third said they had a medical problem. See Maruschak and Beck, 2001, "Medical Problems of Inmates, 1997."

141 D.C. McDonald, "Medical Care in Prisons." In M. Tonry and J. Petersilia (Eds.), *Prisons.* Chicago: University of Chicago Press, 1999. At the same time, some of this may be countered by the possible negative mental health consequences of a period of incarceration.

142 See Maruschak and Beck, 2001, "Medical Problems of Inmates, 1997."

143 See Hammett, 2000, "Health-Related Issues in Prisoner Reentry to the Community."

144 *Ibid.*

145 *Ibid.*

146 *Ibid.*

147 See Ditton, 1999, "Mental Health and Treatment of Inmates and Probationers."

148 See forthcoming Lurigio, "Effective Services for Parolees with Mental Illnesses."

149 See Ditton, 1999, "Mental Health and Treatment of Inmates and Probationers."

150 See forthcoming Lurigio, "Effective Services for Parolees with Mental Illnesses."

151 Mentally ill offenders are more likely than others to be under the influence of alcohol or drugs when they commit an offense.

152 See Hammett, 2000, "Health-Related Issues in Prisoner Reentry to the Community."

153 H.J. Steadman, E.P. Mulvey, J. Monahan, P.C. Robbins, P.S. Appelbaum, T. Grisso, L.H Roth, and E. Silver, "Violence by People Discharged from Acute Psychiatric Inpatient Facilities and by Others in the Same Neighborhoods." *Archives of General Psychiatry*, 55, 1-9, 1998.

154 See Ditton, 1999, "Mental Health and Treatment of Inmates and Probationers."

155 *Ibid.*

156 See forthcoming Lurigio, "Effective Services for Parolees with Mental Illnesses."

157 For a program description, see the Innovations in American Government Web page: http://ksgwww.harvard.edu/innovat/2000/publicheal00.htm. Also, Ted Hammett indicates that a preliminary program analysis found that program participants had lower rates of recidivism than prisoners who did not participate in the program. See Hammett, 2000, "Health-Related Issues in Prisoner Reentry to the Community."

158 J. Kling, D.F. Weiman, and B. Western, "The Labor Market Consequences of 'Mass' Incarceration." Paper prepared for the Reentry Roundtable, Washington, D.C., October 12 and 13, 2000.

159 *Ibid.*

160 Bureau of Justice Statistics, *Survey of State Prison Inmates, 1991.* Washington, D.C.: U.S. Department of Justice, Bureau of Justice Statistics, NCJ 136949, March 1993.

161 S. Bushway, "The Stigma of a Criminal History Record in the Labor Market." In J.P. May (Ed.), *Building Violence: How America's Rush to Incarcerate Creates More Violence.* Thousand Oaks: Sage, 2000.

162 H. Holzer, *What Employers Want: Job Prospects for Less-Educated Workers.* New York: Russell Sage, 1996.

163 See Petersilia, 1999, "Parole and Prisoner Reentry in the United States."

164 See Rottman et al., 2000, "State Court Organization 1998."

165 J. Hagan and R. Dinovitzer, "Collateral Consequences of Imprisonment for Children, Communities, and Prisoners." In M. Tonry and J. Petersilia (Eds.), *Prisons.* Chicago: University of Chicago Press, 1999.

166 *Ibid.*

167 J. Irwin and J. Austin, *It's About Time.* Belmont, CA: Wadsworth, 1994.

168 B. Western and R. Pettit, "Incarceration and Racial Inequality in Men's Employment." *Industrial and Labor Relations Review,* 54, 3-16, 2000.

169 *Ibid.*

170 S. Bushway and P. Reuter, "Labor Markets and Crime." In J.Q. Wilson and J. Petersilia (Eds.), *Crime: Public Policies For Crime Control,* 2nd Edition. San Francisco, CA: ICS Press, forthcoming.

171 See Slambrouck, 2000, "Push to Expand Book-Learning Behind Bars."

172 *Ibid.*

173 Few approaches have proven effective for younger ex-offenders. Ensuring a successful post-prison adjustment for this population remains a challenge. See forthcoming Bushway and Reuter, "Labor Markets and Crime."

174 See Bureau of Justice Statistics, U.S. Department of Justice, 2000, *Correctional Populations in the United States, 1997.*

175 C.G. Camp and G.M. Camp, *The Corrections Yearbook: 1999.* Middletown, CT: Criminal Justice Institute, Inc., 1999.

176 The Welfare to Work Partnership, *Member Survey: Taking the Next Step.* 2000 Series, No. 1.

177 See Gaes et al., 1999, "Adult Correctional Treatment."

178 K.A. Hull, S. Forrester, J. Brown, D. Jobe, and C. McCullen, "Analysis of Recidivism Rates for Participants of the Academic/Vocational/Transition Education Programs Offered by the Virginia Department of Correctional Education." *Journal of Correctional Education,* 51, 2, 256-261, June 2000.

179 S.J. Steurer, L. Smith, A. Tracy. Preliminary analyses of the *Office of Correctional Education and Correctional Education Association Three-State Recidivism Study.* Partial reports from the study will be available soon. See for more information: http://www.ceanational.org/.

180 J. Gerber and E.J. Fritsch, "The Effects of Academic and Vocational Program Participation on Inmate Misconduct and Reincarceration." Ch. 3 in Sam Houston State University, *Prison Education Research Project: Final Report.* Huntsville, TX: Sam Houston State University, 1994.

181 P. Van Slambrouck, "Push to Expand Book-Learning Behind Bars." *The Christian Science Monitor,* September 15, 2000, p. 3.

182 S. Rossman, S. Sridharan, and J. Buck, "The Impact of the Opportunity to Succeed Program on Employment Success." *National Institute of Justice Journal,* 236, July 1998.

183 See program Web site: http://www.ceoworks.org. See National Institute of Justice Web site for program description and evaluation: http://www.ojp.usdoj.gov/reentry/publications.htm.

184 See National Institute of Justice Web site for program description and evaluation: http://www.ojp.usdoj.gov/reentry/publications.htm.

185 See program Web site: http://www.safer-fnd.org. See National Institute of Justice Web site for program description and evaluation: http://www.ojp.usdoj.gov/reentry/publications.htm.

186 See Petersilia, 1999, "Parole and Prisoner Reentry in the United States."

187 Legal Action Center, "Housing Laws Affecting Individuals with Criminal Convictions." Washington, D.C.: Legal Action Center. For more information, see http://www.lac.org/.

188 P.H. Rossi, *Down and Out in America: Origins of Homelessness.* Chicago: University of Chicago Press, 1989.

189 California Department of Corrections, *Preventing Parolee Failure Program: An Evaluation.* Sacramento: California Department of Corrections, 1997.

190 *Ibid.*

191 A recent survey of state statutes identified statutory restrictions on the rights and opportunities of released inmates implemented since the mid-1980s. M. Love and S. Kuzma, *Civil Disabilities of Convicted Felons: A State-by-State Survey.* Washington, D.C.: Office of the Pardon Attorney, 1996. Also see Rottman et al., 2000, "State Court Organization 1998."

192 M. Mauer, *The Race to Incarcerate.* Washington, D.C.: The Prison Project, 2000.

193 Puerto Rico and the following states permanently prohibit convicted felons from voting: Alabama, Arkansas, Delaware, Iowa, Kentucky, Massachusetts, Mississippi, New Mexico, Tennessee, Utah, Virginia, and Washington. While most states have procedures for petitioning the government for reinstatement of voting rights, they can be complicated and in many cases require gubernatorial pardon. See Rottman et al., 2000, "State Court Organization 1998."

194 J. Fellner and M. Mauer, "Losing the Vote: The Impact of Felony Disenfranchisement Laws in the United States." The Sentencing Project, 1998. For more information, see http://www.sentencingproject.org/policy/9080.htm. Also see Mauer, 2000, *The Race to Incarcerate.*

195 See Mauer, 2000, *The Race to Incarcerate.*

196 C.J. Mumola, "Incarcerated Parents and Their Children." Bureau of Justice Statistics, Special Report. Washington, D.C.: U.S. Department of Justice, Bureau of Justice Statistics, NCJ 182335, August 2000.

197 See Beck, 2000, "Prisoners in 1999."

198 See Mumola, 2000, "Incarcerated Parents and Their Children" and C.F. Hairston, "The Forgotten Parent: Understanding the Forces that Influence Incarcerated Fathers' Relationships with Their Children." *Child Welfare* 77, 617-639, 1998.

199 See Mumola, 2000, "Incarcerated Parents and Their Children."

200 See forthcoming Lynch and Sabol, "Prisoner Reentry in Perspective."

[201] See Mumola, 2000, "Incarcerated Parents and Their Children."

[202] Ibid.

[203] See Hagan and Petty, 2000, "Returning Captives of the American War on Drugs: Issues of Community and Family Reentry."

[204] Ibid.

[205] See Mumola, 2000, "Incarcerated Parents and Their Children."

[206] See forthcoming Lynch and Sabol, "Prisoner Reentry in Perspective."

[207] D. Johnston, "Incarceration of Women and Effects on Parenting." Paper presented at a conference on the Effects of Incarceration on Children and Families, Northwestern University, May 5, 2001.

[208] See Mumola, 2000, "Incarcerated Parents and Their Children."

[209] Ibid.

[210] See Hagan and Dinovitzer, 1999, "Collateral Consequences of Imprisonment for Children, Communities, and Prisoners."

[211] See Johnston and Gabel, 1995, "Incarcerated Parents."

[212] Ibid.

[213] D. Johnston, Children of Offenders. Pasadena, CA: Pacific Oaks Center for Children of Incarcerated Parents, 1992. See also D. Johnston, Intergenerational Incarceration. Pasadena, CA: Pacific Oaks Center for Children of Incarcerated Parents, 1993; and D. Johnston, Jailed Mothers. Pasadena, CA: Pacific Oaks Center for Children of Incarcerated Parents, 1991.

[214] C. Seymour, "Children with Parents in Prison: Child Welfare Policy, Program, and Practice Issues." Child Welfare, 77, 5, 469–493, September/October 1998.

[215] Women's Prison Association, "When a Mother is Arrested: How the Criminal Justice and Child Welfare Systems Can Work Together More Effectively." A needs assessment initiated by the Maryland Department of Human Resources, 1996.

[216] See Dallao, 1997, "Coping with Incarceration from the Other Side of the Bars."

[217] C.F. Hairston, "Family Ties During Imprisonment: Important to Whom and for What?" Journal of Sociology and Social Welfare, 18, 87–104, 1991, p. 99.

[218] See Nelson, Deess, and Allen, 1999, The First Month Out: Post-Incarceration Experiences in New York City.

[219] C. Shapiro and M. Schwartz, "Coming Home: Building On Family Connections." Corrections Management Quarterly, forthcoming.

[220] La Bodega de la Familia is about to spin off from the Vera Institute of Justice to become part of Family Justice, a new national nonprofit organization dedicated to the identification, application, and dissemination of best practices in using family supports with individuals under community-based supervision. For more information, see http://www.familyjusticeinc.org.

[221] See Hagan and Petty, 2000, "Returning Captives of the American War on Drugs: Issues of Community and Family Reentry."

[222] Legal Action Center, "Public Assistance Laws Affecting Individuals with Criminal Convictions." Washington, D.C.: Legal Action Center. For more information, see http://www.lac.org/.

[223] See Mumola, 2000, "Incarcerated Parents and Their Children."

[224] See forthcoming Lynch and Sabol, "Prisoner Reentry in Perspective."

[225] Ibid.

[226] Ibid.

[227] Analysis by E. Cadora and C. Swartz for the Community Justice Project at the Center for Alternative Sentencing and Employment Services (CASES), 1999. For more information, see http://www.communityjusticeproject.org/.

[228] Analysis by E. Cadora and C. Swartz for the Community Justice Project at the Center for Alternative Sentencing and Employment Services (CASES), 2001. Based on data from the New York State Division of Parole. For more information, see http://www.communityjusticeproject.org/.

[229] J.P. Lynch and W.J. Sabol, "Prison Use and Social Control." In Criminal Justice: Policies, Processes and Decisions of the Criminal Justice System. Washington, D.C.: U.S. Department of Justice, Office of Justice Programs, National Institute of Justice, 2000.

[230] See forthcoming Lynch and Sabol, "Prisoner Reentry in Perspective."

[231] S. Gottfredson and R. Taylor, "Community Contexts and Criminal Offenders." In T. Hope and M. Shaw (Eds.), Communities and Crime Reduction. London: Home Office, 1988.

[232] T.R. Clear, D.R. Rose, and J.A. Ryder, "Coercive Mobility and the Community: The Impact of Removing and Returning Offenders." Paper prepared for the Reentry Roundtable, Washington, D.C., October 12 and 13, 2000.

[233] Little Hoover Commission, Behind Bars: Correctional Reforms to Lower Prison Costs and Reduce Crime. Sacramento, CA: Little Hoover Commission, 1998.

[234] M.E. Smith and W.J. Dickey, "Reforming Sentencing and Corrections for Just Punishment and Public Safety." Sentencing and Corrections: Issues for the 21st Century, NIJ Research In Brief. Washington, D.C.: National Institute of Justice, September 1999.

[235] J.G. Perry and J.F. Gorczyk, "Restructuring Corrections: Using Market Research in Vermont." Corrections Management Quarterly, 1, 26–35, 1997.

[236] D.M. Kennedy, "Pulling Levers: Chronic Offenders, High-Crime Settings, and a Theory of Prevention." Valparaiso University Law Review, 31, 449–484, 1997.

To receive monthly email updates on Justice Policy Center research,

join the Center's email distribution
list by sending an email to
jpc-requests@ui.urban.org
with the message "subscribe jpc"
in the message body.